THE CASE FOR
CLASSICAL CHRISTIAN EDUCATION

THE CASE FOR
CLASSICAL
CHRISTIAN
EDUCATION

DOUGLAS WILSON

CROSSWAY BOOKS

A DIVISION OF
GOOD NEWS PUBLISHERS
WHEATON, ILLINOIS

The Case for Classical Christian Education

Copyright © 2003 by Douglas Wilson

Published by Crossway Books
        a division of Good News Publishers
        1300 Crescent Street
        Wheaton, Illinois 60187

Cover design: Liita Forsyth

First printing 2003

Printed in the United States of America

Scripture quotations are most often taken from the King James Version of the Bible.

Scripture verses marked ESV are taken from the *Holy Bible: English Standard Version*. Copyright © 2001 by Good News Publishers. Used by permission. All rights reserved.

Library of Congress Cataloging-in-Publication Data
Wilson, Douglas, 1953-
   The case for classical Christian education / Douglas Wilson.
     p. cm.
   Includes bibliographical references and index.
   ISBN 1-58134-384-1
    1. Education, Humanistic—United States. 2. Classical education—
United States. 3. Christian education—United States. I. Title.
LC1023 .W55   2002
370.11'2—dc21   2002002732

BP		13	12	11	10	09	08	07	06	05	04	03
15	14	13	12	11	10	9	8	7	6	5	4	3	2	1

For Nancy,
whose idea it was.

CONTENTS

LIFE IN THE CHRISTIAN SCHOOL

A PROPOSED CURRICULUM

THE DAWN OF EVERLASTING RESULTS

ACKNOWLEDGMENTS

THE PROBLEM WITH acknowledgments in a project of this scope is that I can only acknowledge the extent of my indebtedness without really discharging those debts in any adequate way.

That said, I still want to thank Marvin Olasky for giving me my first opportunity to write on the subject of education. The dedicated board, administration, and staff at Logos School are wonderful Christian people, and it has been an enormous privilege to work with them for so many years. Particular thanks go to Tom Garfield, Tom Spencer, and Matt Whitling. I am grateful to all my colleagues at New St. Andrews College, but particular thanks go to Douglas Jones and Roy Atwood. And thanks also go to Marvin Padgett at Crossway, and to Lila Bishop, my very patient editor. Many thanks also to Mike and Eileen Lawyer for their hard work on the index.

My dear wife, Nancy, is a tireless proofreader. My daughter-in-law Heather Wilson did extraordinary work in her research assistance. Every member of my family is a great blessing to me, and all the work on the subject of education only makes sense because of them—Nancy; Ben and Bekah, with their children Knox, Jemima, and Belphoebe; Nathan and Heather, with their son Rory Douglas; and of course Rachel—or as we call her, the Liz. All three of my children were joyful guinea pigs and wonderful workers, all graduates of Logos and New St. Andrews.

PREFACE

JOHN MILTON, IN HIS great essay on education, said that the task of the educator is to "repair the ruins" created by our first parents Adam and Eve. This phrase has provided the name for our national conferences on educational reform—sponsored by the Association of Classical and Christian Schools—and leads us in turn to a second allusion, which is to the work of Nehemiah, in whose day the Lord gave the people a mind to work. The Israelites had a great wall to rebuild, as do we. We stand in the midst of the rubble of a once-great civilization, and unless God gives us a mind to work, we will all be overwhelmed. We want to build a wall with living stones built into the temple of God.

Over the course of the last twenty years or so, we have addressed many pedagogical issues in many different settings. And we have discovered along the way that the more things change, the more they stay the same. Consequently, I have taken the liberty of quoting in numerous places from other books on education that I have written during the course of our educational pilgrimage. And, as a prophet, one of our own, once put it—"what a long, strange trip it's been."

These citations were included in an attempt to tie various strands of this work together, and not because I really wanted to increase my footnote appearance batting average. Because this is a book that seeks to present a broad overview of the classical Christian model of education, a number of the points made here have already been made elsewhere, scattered around in various books put out by different publishing houses. I thought it better to simply cite those places rather than try to say the same thing again in almost identical words.

When we come to the end of our lives and we consider the work that God gave us to do, it is my hope that the education of our children and grandchildren will occupy a central place in our prayers of gratitude. This book is offered with that end in view.

Douglas Wilson
Christ Church
Moscow, Idaho

ANOTHER BRICK
IN THE WALL

1

A MESS THAT JUST WON'T QUIT

IN ONE SENSE, a good book on education ought to be timeless. God's Word applies equally in all generations, the parents of every age face the same basic task, and children always have the same basic needs. But we live in an era that has been captured by a mind-set that glorifies perpetual revolution—ongoing change merely for the sake of change. Being a progressive is good, even though no one knows what we are progressing *to*. So advocates of classical and Christian education must not only defend their traveling of the old paths, but they must also regularly modify their critique of modern education. Nothing is stranger than a thirty-year-old education fad. Revolutionary education is protean, constantly shifting its external form. But despite the shape-shifting, underneath the surface are the same errors. However, the changes do have the effect of causing the critic's footnotes to become outdated.

When *Recovering the Lost Tools of Learning* was published in 1991, the government school system was in crisis. Some thought that it could not get any worse, but in the time since then, the unthinkable (even for then) has become commonplace. Still many Christians have not yet come to grips with the foundational nature of this crisis. They shake their heads in dismay when they read the newspapers, just as they did in 1991 and 1981 and 1971, but they have not yet realized that the fruit we are seeing is directly related to the nature of the tree. Christian reformers of the government school system labor on, trying to get this crabapple tree to grow oranges. But despite all our advances in genetic engineering, our Lord's words remain—a tree is still known by its fruit. As I said in my book *The Paideia of God:*

A great deal of energy could be preserved if in our reforms we would spend more time trying to identify the genuine point of departure. In the '60s, prayer was banished from the government school system, and the Beatles came to America. Traditional conservatives proved themselves masters of the *post hoc* fallacy and have spent a considerable amount of time, money, and energy trying to get back to the way we were before all that.[1]

We have not yet gotten back to the *status quo ante*, and so it is still necessary to point to the fruit recently produced even though the footnotes on that fruit will be outdated quickly enough. The statistics on education presented here will grow old, but the battle they represent is still part of the perpetual conflict between the seed of the serpent and the seed of the woman. All of this extends back to Eden, and all of it points forward to the future. It is our responsibility as Christian parents and educators to take note of the contemporary details but always to see them in the light of eternity. We live in the present, but are not to be bound to it. We obey (or not) in the present, but our understanding should be captive to the Scriptures, which means that our understanding extends far beyond the immediate crisis. A battle is more than just one sword stroke.

SCHOOL VIOLENCE

Speaking of battle, school shootings and other forms of violence are increasingly common at government schools around the nation. "During 1998 students aged 12 through 18 were victims of more than 2.7 million crimes at school, including about 253,000 serious violent crimes (rape, sexual assault, robbery and aggravated assault)."[2]

The violence threatens everyone, not just the students. It is ongoing and involves far more than just the high-profile murder cases at school. "According to the U.S. Department of Education, from 1994 through 1998, teachers were the victims of approximately 668,000 violent crimes, which include rape or sexual assault, robbery, aggravated assault and simple assault. About 80,000 of those were serious violent crimes."[3]

And while the violence goes far beyond the well-publicized incidents, like the one at Columbine, it certainly includes them. The stories recur with a macabre monotony. After a time it gets harder and harder to distinguish them.

May 21, 1998—Two teenagers are fatally shot, and more than 20 people are hurt when 15-year-old boy allegedly opens fire at a high school in Springfield, Oregon. His parents are found slain at their home. . . .

March 24, 1998—Four girls and a teacher are shot to death, and 10 people are wounded during false fire alarm at a middle school in Jonesboro, Arkansas, when two boys, 11 and 13, open fire from the woods. Both are convicted in juvenile court of murder and can be held up to age 21.[4]

The natural reaction by the general public thus far has been a combination of revulsion and a quick willingness to blame the guns involved. And not surprisingly, the gun issue has become a political football. Among conservative Christians, the defensive response to the uproar over guns has frequently been just as superficial as the attacks—we don't want our guns confiscated, and so we argue that we don't want our guns confiscated.

But we have to do better than this. Who or what is responsible? This radical breakdown of civil order *among our children* is coming from somewhere, and we need to learn the source of it before it overtakes us as well. We are circling the drain, experiencing the downward cycle of sin—and it will do no good to simply find our way back to the previous moment in the cycle. We must be true *radicals*; the word comes from the Latin *radix*, meaning "root." We need to get to the root of the matter. When we discover the source of the problem, we must deal with it thoroughly.

In the nineteenth century, our nation established a socialistic system of education, telling parents that they did not have to exercise the same degree of responsibility for their children that they used to. Lo, and behold, over time parents began to relinquish more and more of their parental duties, assuming that "they" out there somewhere would pick up the slack. Children became increasingly unloved, uncared for, and undisciplined. As the resultant lack of self-control became more evident in schoolchildren, people began to look for alternative means of keeping order. One of the means our modern technocratic society discovered was the ability to hit kids on the head with a chemical rock. As a whole, the government school system has said *yes* to drugs, and students by the thousands found themselves on Ritalin, Prozac, Luvox, Paxil, or other related drugs. In many government school systems, such drugs are actively promoted by the administration as a means of keeping order in the classroom. It is not uncommon for the school to help administer dosages, making sure the kids stay medicated.

But the problem is in one of the potential side effects of many of these drugs. Virtually all of the recent school shootings have been perpetrated by kids on officially sanctioned drugs. Of course, these drugs do not turn every user violent, but they appear to have this effect on a significant number. Kip Kinkel of the Oregon shooting was using Prozac. Eric Harris of the Columbine shooting was taking Luvox, which causes mania in one out of every twenty-five taking it.

Couple this use of drugs with the fact that God and His law are officially and formally ignored in all these educational proceedings. The kids are taught that they evolved from some primordial goo and that their lives have no transcendent meaning. Everything is vanity, everything is worthless. Morality is what you, the student, *want* it to be. And then when some of the kids, natural inhibitions loosened by the drugs, take this curricular lesson out to the logical practicum and start blowing fellow students away, bits of protoplasm every one of them, those in authority wonder where this behavior is coming from.

The kids who turn violent are called "monsters" by the school system that made them what they are. Instead of shrinking back from the logic of the conclusion, schools should give these kids honorary diplomas. These students, at least, have understood what they were being taught.

We had plenty of guns long before these shootings started. Our civil disintegration in the schools is the clear result of two principal factors: Our children are under-disciplined and overmedicated.

So the problem is obvious. But it is equally obvious that those in authority have no intention of seeing the obvious. The solution, they solemnly maintain with a straight face, is trigger locks and other forms of gun control. But we do not need gun control; we need self-control. And we cannot have self-control, a fruit of the Spirit, without the Gospel.

Christian parents therefore have a broad responsibility to our civil order. There are a number of specific things that can be done, and the purpose of this book is to encourage Christian parents already engaged in the task and to motivate other Christian parents to begin their involvement, particularly as it concerns our children.

Under our current circumstances, the first action to take, if it applies, is for parents to pull their own children out of the government school system and never think about putting them back in. The first motive for doing this is the protection (spiritual, covenantal, academic, etc.) of the children. The second motive is the protection of those children who remain behind. The sooner the *current* government school system collapses, the better it will be for everyone, including those who were enrolled at the time the schools fell apart.

The second course of action is to talk at every opportunity about the spiritual and cultural malaise that pervades the culture our young people are growing up in and how the entrenched education establishment is trying to hide this rapidly escalating problem by inducing brain fog in any children who act up. In private conversation, in letters to the editor, and anywhere else we have the opportunity, we need to be wondering loudly about this gross dereliction of public responsibility. The broad responsibility for school shootings has to be laid squarely at the feet of our modern educrats. But we ought not to wait for them to get our point and change.

The third action people can take is to build an alternative educational subculture. This means planting and building schools. Children in our classical Christian academies are not aliens; they are modern American kids. And as outsiders see what it is possible for a modern American kid to be and do, they will start to see the lie they have been sold. But it is important that the private schools we start not imitate in any fundamental way the pedagogy of the government school system, the god that failed.

JUST SAY *YES* TO DRUGS

Our much hooplahed "war on drugs" has actually been what might be called a war on free-market drug use. Regulated and officially administered drugs are a different matter. The Drug-Free Zone sign outside many of our government schools is laughable once we consider the facts.

Despite decades of official warnings and supporting research confirming the similarities of methylphenidate (Ritalin) and cocaine, tens of millions of children in the United States have been prescribed this psychotropic drug for a widely accepted yet scientifically unproved mental condition: Attention-Deficit/Hyperactivity Disorder (ADHD).

Now a recently concluded study at the Brookhaven National Laboratory (BNL) not only confirms the similarities of cocaine and Ritalin, but finds that Ritalin is more potent than cocaine in its effect on the dopamine system, which many doctors believe is one of the areas of the brain most affected by drugs such as Ritalin and cocaine. The outcome of the research was so surprising that team leader Nora Volkow, a psychiatrist who is associate laboratory director for life sciences at BNL, told the media that she and the team were "shocked as ____ " at the results.[5]

Such is our condition that more Christian parents are likely to be shocked at the researcher's use of profanity than they are at the fact of this massive use of chemical discipline. How massive? The story continues: "The most recent figures available reveal that in 1998 there were approximately 46 million children in kindergarten through grade 12. Twenty percent—one of every five children in school—have been doped with the mind-altering drug."[6] Twenty percent. We have a way to go before we get to Huxley's *Brave New World*, but "better living" through chemistry nevertheless appears to be one of our driving principles.

And this situation illustrates the nature of our dilemma. Suppose for a moment that some prophet had come out of the wilderness in 1958 and predicted that within a generation one-fifth of the children enrolled in our schools would be doped into docility. The prophet would, of course, have been laughed back to his cave. Yet the spiritual nature of our disease is such that when these things do come to pass, precisely because they *have* come to pass, it is impossible to see them. Before they happen, we cannot see them because they have not yet happened. After they happen, we cannot see them because we *let* them happen, and seeing would now require repentance.

In another context, William Bennett has written about the death of outrage in our culture. But the spiritual malaise in which we find ourselves has more than one symptom. Our inability to get angry at what is being done to our children is not an intellectual problem. At bottom the massive abdication of responsibility is a spiritual issue. But because we have accepted the propaganda of pluralism, we think that all we need to do is maintain our opinions and simply state them as such, and we are therefore exempted from all negative consequences. We think that in a pluralistic society it is possible for a person to reap something other than what he or she has sown. Our ready acceptance of the excuses offered by the government school establishment reminds me of the title of one of Dilbert's insightful books—*When Did Ignorance Become a Point of View?*

But, we are told, the children have to receive these drugs in order to deal with their learning disabilities. And so this brings us to consider the academic state of the schools. Such is the state of our education system that before we could offer a critique of actual learning in the schools, we had to first deal with the possibilities of children getting shot and with students being drugged by the school nurse—employed full time for that purpose.

HOW IT IS THAT JOHNNY STILL DOESN'T LEARN

No one should be surprised to hear that the academic state of the government schools remains dismal. In the last presidential campaign, George Bush ran on a pledge to help "every child learn to read by third grade." As he put it: "There's too many of our kids in America who can't read today. . . . Now it's time to wage war on illiteracy for the young and to whip this problem early."[7]

Early? Literacy by third grade is *early*? As the ongoing problem with illiteracy in the schools continues to plague us, politicians will continue to call for more programs to fight it. Of course, some of us are a bit slow about these things. We thought that *schools* were supposed to be the program to fight illiteracy.

According to "The Nation's Report Card," "In 2000, the percentage of fourth-grade students performing at or above the Basic level of reading achievement was 63 percent. Performance at or above the Proficient level—the level identified by NAGB as the level that all students should reach—was achieved by 32 percent of fourth-graders."[8] In simple English, when it comes to literacy, one-third of fourth graders were at the place where all fourth graders should be.

Not surprisingly, our problems are not limited to reading. ABC News reported that nationally "only 23 percent of eighth graders tested 'proficient' in math. Thirty-nine percent tested below even the 'basic' level."[9] "American 12th graders came in 19th out of 21 countries in mathematics on the Third International Mathematics and Science Study (TIMSS), besting only Cyprus and South Africa. The U.S. came in last in advanced mathematics. In physics, 12th graders did equally as poorly."[10]

Our academic decline is not limited to what we would consider poor students. The decline affects our top students as well. The *Washington Post* comments: "Even the scores of academically elite American students—those who take either physics or advanced math courses in high school—were a disappointment. They also finished below the international average and lagged behind many other nations on the latest test."[11]

A recent report from the Department of Education—the 2001 History Report Card—was genuinely alarming. This report, coming from a source hardly hostile to the idea of public education, detailed "truly abysmal scores" from U.S. high school seniors. Fifty-seven percent of the seniors could not perform at the most basic level. Thirty-two percent were at the basic level. Ten percent performed at grade level on the test, and one percent were advanced or superior. George Washington? Who's that?[12]

While academic performance is falling apart, what are students doing to fill up their time? Not surprisingly, "59.4 percent of 8th grade (age 13) students watch television three to four hours or more a day. Of these students, 12 percent report watching six or more hours a day."[13]

Many hours of slack-jaw entertainment cannot be good for the cultivation of academic rigor. But it would be too facile to say that television *necessarily* turns the brain to mush, and that this is why the students are doing poorly. But at the very least we can say that the three or four hours of watching the tube are hours in which homework is not being done. And all this wasted time is related to another factor—lack of adult supervision. "Nearly 7.5 million children ages 5-14 are on their own in the morning and afternoon before and after the school bell rings. Nearly two-thirds of school-age children are in homes with working parents."[14]

But not all is doom and gloom. Occasionally the government school establishment is cheered by a report that best fits in the category of "not exactly *bad* news." Sometimes SAT tests go up a point or so, and while any slight increase is certainly more welcome than a finger in the eye, it is not yet time to start doing handstands. Despite glitches here and there, the scores are consistently low, and nothing has occurred to indicate the trend is reversed.

An (apparently) unrelated story was the Gallup poll of a few years back that indicated that a significant majority of Americans, 68 percent, strongly favor the distribution of condoms in the government schools. That number was divided between the 43 percent who said condoms should be given to any students who want them and the 25 percent who thought that the schools should require parental consent.

What may arguably tie these statistics together is the apparently missing factor everywhere—parents. Competent educators have long known that one of the most important assets a child has in his education is the involvement of parents. And pastors have long known that parental oversight of the sexual development of their children is one of the central keys to a future well-adjusted marriage for those children.

Each round of SAT scores brings a number of old recurring pedagogical debates to the surface again. Educators have long been debating whether the SAT tests are an accurate assessment of how we educate. Some think the tests are just fine and that we ought not to shoot the messenger for bringing us bad news. Others complain that the tests are biased against minorities, and still others maintain that the tests should be geared more to the testing of achievement rather than ability. But while tinkering with the tests may squeeze a few points out of them here and there, the fundamental problem of parental abdication remains. Altering and improving the tests cannot get parents involved. *That* cannot be done without altering our entire system of education.

But back to the condoms. Among those favoring condom distribution, 43 percent thought the parents ought not to be involved at all, and the remaining 25 percent were only looking to the parents for the final okay. None of the 68 percent appeared to think that parents should oversee, from beginning to end, the sexual maturing of their children.

When test scores are poor, there is still an expectation that the schools must fix the problem—instead of demanding that the schools get out of the way so the parents and their true servants in private schools can fix it. And when sexual disease, illegitimate pregnancy, AIDS, and abortion afflict our teenagers, there is still widespread support for giving the job of fixing *that* to our schools as well.

So none of this should be a great surprise. If parents leave their kids standing alone on a street corner long enough, it is simply a matter of time before someone offers them a condom. Or a lousy education.

THROWING MONEY AT IT

But a lousy education need not be a *cheap* education. Critics of the government schools know it is not possible to criticize them without hearing the reply that the problem is lack of funding. But this is *hturt*—the truth with dyslexia. The current expenditure per pupil in average daily attendance in public elementary and secondary schools (1999-2000) was $7,086. In *adjusted* dollars, the expenditure for 1961-62 was $2,360. While we are at it, to illustrate another problem we have the dishonesty of inflation. In unadjusted dollars the cost per pupil in 1961 was $419.[15] Put simply, we are spending three times as much per pupil in constant dollars as we were then, and we are getting far, far less for all that extra money.

To illustrate, assume that a gallon of milk sold for $1.00 in 1961. Say that today it costs $3.00, but it is no longer a gallon but rather a half-gallon. In real terms, this is a sixfold increase. And the analogy still breaks down because with a half-gallon of milk, you still get *milk*. With our education system today, we get less education, and then in the "education" we do receive, we find that the milk is well-watered. In my book *Excused Absence* I pointed out the futility of trying to reform this system:

> The system of education we have in this country is *unworkable*. Why do we keep trying to make it work? The answer is that God has turned us over to our folly. He is the one who gives us statutes that are not good (forced bussing, whole language instruction, Outcome-Based Education, sex education for tots, *ad infinitum*). We complain under these judgments, but complaining is not the same as repentance.[16]

I was not blaming God for our folly but simply recognizing that God uses our follies to chastise us. God is not mocked. Paul says that a man reaps what he sows (Gal. 6:7).

Our problem in the schools is by no means the result of a lack of funds. The government school system has enormous amounts of money, and it is doing extraordinarily foolish things with it. What might some of those things be?

WHILE ROME BURNS

The government school system is successful. These schools are only a failure if one measures failure in terms of illiteracy. The fact that the system is unsuccessful at true *education* is merely a distraction. In all things to which our government educators are truly committed, they have had remarkable success. We need only look at the arena of overhauling our public and cultural expectations in the next generation. The following goals are excerpted from the NEA resolutions passed at the 2001 Convention in Los Angeles: "A-13. Financial Support of Public Education. Funds must be provided for programs to alleviate race, gender, and sexual orientation discrimination and to eliminate portrayal of race, gender, and sexual orientation stereotypes in the public schools."[17]

We are not a more literate society than we were ten years ago. But are we more or less committed to *this* particular goal? What has been the success of the gay activist agenda in the last ten years? These people know what they are doing.

> B-9. Racism, Sexism, and Sexual Orientation Discrimination. Discrimination and stereotyping based on such factors as race, gender, immigration status, disability, ethnicity, occupation, and sexual orientation must be eliminated. Plans, activities, and programs must . . . increase respect, understanding, acceptance, and sensitivity toward gays, lesbians, bisexuals, transgendered people.[18]

If we are numbered among those who believe that "gays, lesbians, bisexuals, transgendered people" must be called to repentance, the goals of the NEA should be recognized for what they are. We "*must* increase respect, understanding, acceptance, and sensitivity" toward them regardless of what Scripture says. But still many Christians thoughtlessly send their children off to be educated by these people.

"B-1. Early Childhood Education. The National Education Association supports early childhood education programs in the public schools for children from birth through age eight."[19] But the work of these educators is still difficult because the first five years of a child's life (lived in a Christian home) creates more resistance than they would like (although far *less* than I would like). And so they want government education programs for *newborns* on up to age eight. This is not because the education bureaucracy is tender toward little ones. Far from it.

"I-12. Family Planning. The National Education Association supports family planning, including the right to reproductive freedom. The Association also urges the implementation of community-operated, school-based family planning clinics that will provide intensive counseling by trained personnel."[20] Christians accustomed to the pro-choice world of euphemisms recognize what is proposed here. Reproductive freedom is the freedom to abort an unborn child. Family-planning clinics are places that arrange for abortions or provide them directly. The NEA wants such clinics to be school-based. At the end of this particular road, we will find that the phrase *school violence* will take on an even ghastlier meaning.

The NEA knows what it wants and is willing to dedicate its resources to get it. Sad to say, on the other hand, most Christian parents do not know what they want and are not willing to sacrifice anything. Many within the system still have a biblical view of morality, and so they want to work against this sinful agenda and try to restore "traditional" morality to American schools.

> On what moral basis shall the teacher who wholly suppresses all appeal to religion rest that authority which he must exercise in the classroom? He will find it necessary to say to the pupil, "Be diligent. Be obedient. Do not lie." This must be done so the student may acquire his secular knowledge. But on whose authority? By what standard?[21]

Education is fundamentally religious. Consequently, there is no question about *whether* a morality will be imposed in that education, but rather *which* morality will be imposed. Christians and assorted traditionalists who want a secular school system to instill anything other than secular ethics are wanting something that has never happened and can never happen.

> Because all truths converge towards God, the teacher who cannot name God must have fragmented teaching. He can only construct a truncated figure. In history, ethics, philosophy and jurisprudence, religious facts and propositions are absolutely inseparable from the subject at hand. The necessary discipline of a schoolroom and secular fidelity of teaching require religion.[22]

If they converge toward the Christian God, then He will be acknowledged, and His Word will be honored. If all "truths" converge on the Sinai of another god, then we will see his law/word imposed. And that "law" will in our day amount to some variation of catering to established powers that be.

SO HERE WE ARE, STILL

We have been told many times that the one thing we learn from history is that we do not learn from history. This axiom appears to be true in many settings, but one area where it is manifestly the case is in the history of tax-supported education in America for the last 150 years. The one type of person who cannot be educated appears to be the American education professional.

But this is just an appearance. Consider the textbook case of the failure to teach literacy. Is this not a true failure? This is a failure only if literacy were the goal. But if the true goals were power and money, then the story is a little different. As always, *follow the money*.

A "new method" for learning to read was proposed by Horace Mann in 1837. He got it from Thomas Gallaudet, who had developed a way to teach reading to deaf children who couldn't sound anything out. This "look-say" method was tried for a few years in Boston and then abandoned. Many educators still had the idea that education was the goal, and so they objected when that goal was threatened. The "look-say" method was to replace the older method of teaching children the phonetic sounds of letters and combinations of letters—which worked quite well.

In 1930 "basal readers" were introduced that had the support of John Dewey. The pedagogy behind this new teaching method is called by many names, but the rejection of phonetic instruction is at the foundation of them all. According to Robert Sweet, "One philosophy of teaching reading is usually called 'whole language,' but many other labels are used to describe it, such as the whole-word method, language experience, psycholinguistics, look and say, reading recovery, balanced literacy, or integrated reading instruction."[23]

The failure of this method in teaching children to read has been spectacular. But measured another way, the story is different. This "whole-language" method has *not* failed to bring money into the coffers of the government education system. Success or failure is all a matter of what you are trying to do. Basal readers are much more expensive than phonics materials (by about four times), and an entire industry has grown up around providing them to the schools. The government schools will stop what they are doing when the American taxpayer stops giving them raises for doing it.

But in the meantime, they do have to answer their critics, and so they have many varied responses:

> Since admitting fault is not an easy thing for anyone to do, most education professionals respond to research findings that advocate the teaching of intensive systematic phonics with the following excuses: There isn't an illiteracy problem; we do teach phonics; no one method is best; English isn't phonetic; word calling isn't reading; the child isn't ready; the child has a reading disability; it's the parents' fault; it's too much TV.[24]

But what is the true goal? If it is the accumulation of power and influence, then nothing succeeds like failure. "Reading failure usually shows up after the fourth grade when the volume of words needed for reading more difficult materials in science, literature, history, or math cannot be memorized quickly enough."[25] In other words, the educational disaster that has come from whole-language instruction is not readily apparent when it is first implemented in the first grade. But a few years later, the concrete is dry, and the damage is done.

When the failure of whole-language becomes apparent, what do we do? Change? Go back to older teaching methods? Not at all—we press on to the goal. We ask for more funding because we now need special programs to help these kids with learning disabilities.

THE LAY OF THE LAND

The problem is so evident that it is sometimes exasperating to see how slowly Christian parents in our nation have caught on. But many have. Finally.

> Statistics that reflect the years 1995-2000 indicate that the U.S. has 115,921 elementary and secondary schools. Of these 88,519 are government schools, and 27,402 are private. The number of students enrolled is approximately 52 million, with 46 million still in government schools, 5.9 million in private academies, and about 1.7 million being homeschooled.[26]

A significant minority of parents have said that they are not interested in having the government make any more money off their educational malpractice with children. About seven and a half million children have been removed from the system to date. Further, these estimates are likely low, given the lack of interest that many parents and school administrators have in telling the government what they are up to or where they went. In my community, the public bafflement over the declining enrollment in the government schools has been actually amusing to watch. Twenty years ago when Logos School started, less than 5 percent of the children in our community were privately educated. Now the figure is around 30 percent. But the public school officials are so unused to competition that if public school enrollment decreases, they assume that the only possible reason is that the birth rate in the community has decreased.

Sabbath Rest

And so this book is a call to continued reformation of education in our country. But a warning at the very beginning is in order. Americans tend to want their reformations the same way they want their coffee—hot and now.

When we decide what we want, we scramble to get it. Look around for a moment at life in contemporary America. In every direction, we see a full-tilt, frenetic pace of life, meaning that everyone is on the go. And when we get wherever it is we are going, we find the place open twenty-four hours, seven days a week. If we were to hit the freeway at four in the morning, we would not find ourselves alone. A multitude of other early risers would all be off to somewhere important.

Americans are workers, and of course this is not a bad thing in itself. Work is necessary and good. Our problem is that the work we do is not undergirded with any sense of *rest*. The end result of this attitude is a culture-wide frazzled tangle of stressed-out nerve endings. And when we react to the frazzle, we too often do so in a frazzled way. When we respond to the failures of modern education, we do so in a way that is a pale shadow of that failure, instead of providing a genuine alternative.

Although this may sound odd to modern ears, the reason we have drifted into this frantic lifestyle is largely theological. We do not comprehend physical rest because we have no spiritual rest. And we have no spiritual rest because we do not understand that salvation is by grace and not by works: "For by grace are ye saved through faith; and that not of yourselves: it is the gift of God: Not of works, lest any man should boast" (Eph. 2:8-9).

The Bible portrays salvation in terms of complete rest. This includes the salvation of our children and of the schools they attend. The only reason the rest can be complete is that it is a gift from God. We do not have the ability to earn even the smallest portion of it. God offers the gift of salvation rest, and the reason men and women fall short of it is because of their unbelief (Heb. 3:19—4:2). But whenever we hear the promises concerning salvation in the Bible, we must hear those words in faith if they are to bring us any rest at all. And lest we fall into the temptation of thinking that faith is simply a "tiny work" that we must do, God also tells us that faith is part of His gift to us as well.

But the faith He gives to us is not a blind faith—it is not a "letting go" so that we might fall into some spiritual void. Rather it is a response to what God has done in history. Specifically, we must remember that Jesus Christ died on the cross in order to purchase forgiveness for His people and that He rose again from the dead so that we could participate in His everlasting life. That new life, the Bible says, is a life of *rest*.

In an important sense, every culture is the externalization of some religion. And every school exists to perpetuate and pass on that culture. As we look around at that great squirrel-cage run we call modernity, we see that most of us as moderns belong to a religion called Getting Ahead. In contrast to this attitude, Jesus issued a wonderful invitation: "Take my yoke upon you, and learn of me; for I am meek and lowly in heart; and ye shall find rest unto your souls" (Matt. 11:29).

True education reform begins in rest; it begins with grace. We cannot hope to be effective in this work unless we get the Gospel straight and, having gotten it straight, rest in the promises given. Contrary to the opinions of our adversaries, education is not a savior. But it can be saved.

2

THE RISE AND FALL OF SECULAR EDUCATION IN AMERICA

GOVERNMENT EDUCATION IN America cannot be understood apart from democracy. And the rise and fall of secular education in this nation cannot be comprehended without understanding the rise and fall of democracy.

Because we always tend to heal the wound lightly, we want to think that everything was all right until the 1950s, but then everything fell apart suddenly and mysteriously. But our problem goes down to the bone. As I stated in my book *Repairing the Ruins:* "Some of us wistfully look back to the government schools of our childhood, back before prayer was banned. *If only . . .* This nostalgic approach neglects one thing—the government schools were a rebellious idea from the start."[1]

The nature of this rebellion was democracy—the rule of *demos*, the people. The people *en masse* were thought of as having final authority—over traditions, kings, customs, historic loyalties, and churches. We have grown accustomed to thinking of our democracy as a good thing, and it surprises us to learn that the founding fathers of our nation were deeply suspicious of democracy and tried to place whatever restraints on it they could. They established a constitutional republic, not a democracy, and it is a sign of our current ignorance that we do not even know the difference between the two.

This democratic impulse exploded into full revolt near the beginning of the nineteenth century, and three significant columns began to march on the older established order of Christendom. The political revolution was accomplished in the election of Andrew Jackson to the presidency in 1829. The ecclesiastical revolution was ushered in during the Second

Great Awakening, beginning on the Kentucky frontier in 1799 and spreading through ardent revivalist preachers such as Charles Finney in the early decades of that century. The educational revolution was led by Horace Mann, who was dedicated to bringing this democratic "gospel" to the children in order to perpetuate that democratic order to future generations.

All three movements were related to one another and were manifestations of this newly-minted faith in man, the democratic *zeitgeist*. At the beginning, this faith was full of robust enthusiasm and was not at all shy or reluctant about imposing democratic standards, relying on the abundant capital inherited from the older Christian order. The prodigal son did not run out of money on his first day away from home. The democratic institutions established at that time were rigorous, and those who were content to look at short-term results could readily be impressed. For a time, when the prodigal was buying drinks for the house, he looked like a wealthy man.

Today some are called educational reformers simply because they want to go back to that earlier rigor. A good example is Mortimer Adler, who was responsible for the establishment of the well-respected Great Books curriculum and who could hardly be accused of supporting low standards in education. But Adler understood and acknowledged his basic intellectual commitments: "The first and most important distinguishing characteristic of *The Paideia Proposal* is that it takes democracy seriously."[2]

In addition, he acknowledged his historical predecessors.

> My book, *The Paideia Proposal*, is dedicated to Horace Mann, John Dewey, and Robert Hutchins. To Horace Mann because in the middle of the last century he struggled valiantly to see that on the eastern seaboard the children had at least six years of free compulsory schooling.... To John Dewey because, in 1916, in his book, *Democracy and Education*, Dewey put those two words together for the first time in history. By doing so, he showed that in our kind of society, all the children who go to school are destined to have the same kind of future; therefore, the objectives of the schooling should be the same for all. They should all have exactly the same quality of schooling. And to Robert Hutchins for a single sentence that sums it all up: "The best education for the best is the best education for all."[3]

Adler was a committed democrat. As he put it, *"The Paideia Proposal* was dedicated to these men because of their commitment to a democratic system of education."[4] At the same time, Adler was truly committed to high standards. He wanted to return to the time when democracy could plausibly promise to provide an education for all. But despite the best efforts of reformers like Adler, turning the clock back does not constitute true reform. If a man were to rent a video, and it turned out to be a poor movie, it is not "movie reform" to rewind and try again.

Adler's approach to education was democratic because of where his faith was placed. A Christian desires to bring education to all, but not because every person is inherently good and deserves to be educated. Rather, all people are sinners, but the grace of God has been revealed to us, and we should want to teach all people so that they might come to salvation and grow in their gratitude to God for His grace. But the democrat places his faith in man, and the provision of education is a matter of *justice*, not a matter of kindness and grace. To quote Adler again: "What I do have a right to is help from the state in gaining knowledge. *I have a right* to schooling. I am deprived if I am deprived of schooling."[5]

Writer Christopher Dawson has a firmer grasp of the parasitic nature of American democracy in the realm of education:

> The forefather of modern education, who was more consistent than his descendants, Jean Jacques Rousseau, would perhaps have approved of this [socialized primitivism], since he believed that civilization was on the whole a mistake and that man would be better without it. But the modern democrat usually has a rather naive faith in modern civilization, and he wishes to accept the inheritance of culture, while rejecting the painful process of social and intellectual discipline by which that inheritance has been acquired and transmitted.[6]

In other words, the fruit of many centuries of patient Christian cultivation was assumed by the educational democrats to be something that happened in spite of Christianity. The fruit had arrived, mysteriously, because a new age had dawned, and all we needed to do was consistently extend our faith in man into everything. The optimism of these men and their messianic fervor was boundless. As Horace Mann put it:

> The question for us is, has not the fullness of time NOW come? Are not the sufferings of past ages, are not the cries of expiring nations, whose echoes have not yet died away, a summons sufficiently loud to reach our ears, and to rouse us to apply a remedy for the present, an antidote for

the future? We shall answer these questions, by the way in which we educate the rising generation.[7]

Note the messianic language here—the "fullness of time" actually arrived when Christ came to redeem His people. But now here in North America, at last the educators had arrived to eliminate human suffering. Mann elsewhere claimed that the common schools would usher in a virtual utopia with crime almost eradicated.

This was the wave of the future, and it swept through the West. "Everywhere the control of education passed from the Church to the State, and in many countries the rights of the teaching orders to conduct their own schools and colleges was limited or denied."[8] Dawson goes on to cite two surviving exceptions—England and the United States. They were exceptions only in the fact that private teaching was still *legal*. But the center had shifted even in these two countries.

These movers and shakers in the world of American education "reform" were consistently hostile to orthodox Christianity. But the local government schools were often run by Christians who did not know what was being done to them at the higher levels. Because Christians controlled the schools locally and because their communities were evangelical, so were the schools. But certain far-sighted Christian thinkers saw what was happening and warned about the coming consequences. One of the prophetic voices belonged to R. L. Dabney. "We have seen that their [the schools'] complete secularization is logically inevitable. Christians must prepare themselves then, for the following results: All prayer, catechisms, and Bibles will ultimately be driven out of the schools."[9]

Dabney spoke these words in the nineteenth century, long before prayer was finally banned in the 1960s. I can still remember what it was like praying in the government school I attended as a child. But I don't remember any Bibles, and I certainly don't remember any catechisms. When Dabney predicted the final victory of the secularists, the schools on the ground were locally controlled by Christians; Bibles, prayers, and catechisms were all part of the curriculum. Dabney said what he did because the secularists had already established their victory *in principle*. The Christians who were involved in the common schools at that time were attempting to have it both ways. They wanted their Christian fruit to grow on a secularist tree.

Dabney saw this contradiction, but he also knew that secular education was a contradiction in terms.

> So is a really secularized education either possible or admissible? Before ours, no people of any age, religion, or civilization, has ever thought so. Against the present attempt, right or wrong, stands the whole common sense of mankind. Pagans, Catholics, Moslems, Greeks and Protestants have all rejected any education not grounded in religion as absurd and wicked.[10]

It was absurd *and* impossible. Consequently, the attempt to establish secular education was really an attempt to supplant one type of religious education with the education of another competing religion. The pretense of neutrality was exactly that—a pretense. God was to be toppled, and a new god, the god *demos*, was to be honored in His place. This revolution was possible because the Christians of that time were confused about what was actually happening. Tragically, this confusion remains with many believers down to the present.

> It must be acknowledged to be one of the most remarkable phenomena of our perverted humanity, that among a Christian people, and in a Protestant land, such a discussion [whether the education of youth may be secularized] should not seem as absurd as to inquire whether schoolrooms should be located under water or in dark caverns! The Jew, the Moslem, the follower of Confucius, and of Brahma, each and all are careful to instruct the youth of their people in the tenets of the religions they profess, and are not content until, by direct and reiterated teaching, they have been acquainted with at least the outline of the books which contain, according to their beliefs, the revealed will of God. Why are Christians so indifferent to such an obvious duty, which is so obviously recognized by Jew and pagan?[11]

Education is a religious endeavor for every student. "Make that godless, and his life is made godless."[12] In the nineteenth century, secular education was established because many Christians were fatally persuaded of the myth of neutrality. They were told that there were many areas of life that could be studied apart from any reference to the authority of Scripture. They accepted the pluralistic nature of American public life, not as a social reality requiring intensive missionary activity, but rather as an authoritative voice, requiring every practitioner of every religion to submit and fit in.

And this is why even today we hear "pluralism" as a code word requiring Christians to shut up. Of course, we are a pluralistic country. And ancient Rome was a pluralistic empire, but Jesus still told His disciples to preach the Gospel there.

Properly understood, pluralism is simply another name for polytheism. When we say "pluralism," what does the plurality refer to? The answer is, to a plurality of authoritative voices, the Babel of competing divine voices, all saying what we ought to do. Because this situation creates a potential for civic trouble, the powers that be impose certain conditions on the devotees of all these religions: "You may believe and practice as you please, so long as you demonstrate your willingness to tolerate the gods worshiped by your neighbors. You will demonstrate this by burning incense to the genius of the emperor." Or in our case, we have to demonstrate our tamed status by agreeing that pluralism is a wonderful thing—which many Christian leaders continue to do. But such idolatrous compromise is precisely what the early Christians refused to do, and this is precisely why they were persecuted.

Christian education cannot be sustained apart from the exclusive worship of the triune God. And such worship cannot be offered to Him and to *demos*. He will not accept it, and, incidentally, neither will *demos*. The establishment of a Christian school movement is in principle a threat to the current establishment, and the establishment knows it.

This chapter title referred to the rise and fall of secular education. The rise of secular education in our nation corresponded to the rise of our faith in democracy. It will not fall, however bad the test scores get, until that fundamental faith is rattled and abandoned in repentance. There are some indications that this is starting to happen. It has not yet occurred, but one still hopes.

3

HEALING THE WOUND LIGHTLY

FOR MANY AMERICANS, some system of tax-supported education is simply a given. As unquestioned assumptions go, this one ranks near the top. The power of this idea can be seen in the responses to the increasingly obvious failure of the government school system. The first response, a religious one, is always to call for reform. There are differences, however. The reformers are divided as to whether the impetus to such reform should come from within the school system or without.

Those who press for the reinstitution of prayer in schools or the elimination of offensive textbooks, or other similar issues, want to bring the government schools back to a more traditional center. Those who argue for vouchers, or to a lesser extent charter schools, are trying to reform the government schools from the outside. They want to bring the pressure of honest competition to bear, and then in the light of that external competition, let the government schools themselves decide what they should do.

But in both cases, the desire is for reform to take hold in order to save the schools. This goal is related to the deep commitment to democracy mentioned earlier. We have not yet learned that democracy is the problem. In his discussion of education, Mortimer Adler provides a good example of this fundamental religious commitment: "I assume, without any argument at all, that we are committed to a democratic society, a democratic government, and democratic institutions. And I assume that this means the acceptance of the basic truth of human equality, which expresses itself in the political principle of universal suffrage."[1]

With this commitment as a starting assumption, the only question concerns how our "public schools" should be managed and not whether we should have them in the first place. For Adler, the question of abolishing government-supported education is as unthinkable as firing all the policemen.

> These general truths of political philosophy determine the proper role of public education as a political institution. Along with law enforcement agencies, public health services, military forces, the educational system is one of the instrumentalities of government, and in a sense the most important because it is entirely positive and constructive in its operation. All of these implements of government are well employed only if they are directed to the ends which government itself must serve, in order to be just, namely, the common good immediately and the happiness of men ultimately.[2]

The advocates of internal reform in the government schools have accepted this fundamental assumption, and as participants in this vast democracy, they want to use their presence to *influence* events in a particular direction. They want stricter discipline, higher academic standards, uniforms, school prayer, and so forth. The issue here is a specific kind of worldview problem.

The Christian faith is not a condiment to be used to flavor the neutral substance of secular knowledge. Paul tells us that every thought is to be made captive to Christ (2 Cor. 10:1-4). Christ says that anyone who does not gather with Him is scattering (Matt. 12:30). The Christian faith does very poorly as mere decorative material. Jesus said that we are to disciple the nations, and to the extent that we see anything out of line with His Word, we are to call that into obedience. J. Gresham Machen made the point with characteristic clarity and insight and is worth quoting at length:

> Furthermore, the field of Christianity is the world. The Christian cannot be satisfied so long as any human activity is either opposed to Christianity or out of all connection with Christianity. Christianity must pervade not merely all nations, but also all of human thought. The Christian, therefore, cannot be indifferent to any branch of earnest human endeavor. It must all be brought into *some* relation to the gospel. It must be studied either in order to be demonstrated as false, or else in order to be made useful in advancing the Kingdom of God. The Kingdom must be advanced not merely extensively, but also intensively. The Church must seek to conquer not merely every man for Christ, but also the whole of man.[3]

The longer the Christian faith is *used* as though it were a condiment, the less like the faith of our fathers it becomes. We see this process at work in the discussions over school prayer. To whom would the children be praying? To the true God? If the prayer in question is being offered to the God of Abraham, the Father of our Lord Jesus Christ, then does not honesty require us to say so and to mention His name in the prayer and conclude the prayer in the name of Jesus?

But if the prayer is being offered to *another* god, then why are Christians trying to promote it? It should be obvious that Christians should not proselytize on behalf of another faith. Christian churches would not send out Muslim missionaries.

What is actually happening is a good deal more confusing than either of these clear options, but in effect it still amounts to the latter. The "god" being addressed in all such prayers is the generic god of American civil religion. Christians assume that this is not idolatrous prayer because the word *god* serves as a holding tank into which members of different faiths can put the content of their individual theologies. Everyone's faith, the thinking goes, is flexible enough to do this except for the faith of intransigent atheists—or consistent Christians. The god of American civil religion is a supreme being who has been defined in multiple court cases as non-triune—he is not the God of the Scriptures. Therefore, Christians have a moral responsibility *not* to offer incense on that altar and still less to try to get others to do so.

School prayer is the most "spiritual" of attempted reforms from within the system, and ironically it is therefore the most disobedient. Tightening up discipline and reducing crime in the hallways can be understood as a manifestation of common grace. Christians can support the efforts it takes to keep citizens from being murdered anywhere, and this would of course include the schools. But prayer is a form of worship. If it is not Christian prayer, then it is idolatrous prayer. The "common grace" reforms, however, do become a problem when they are advocated so that Christian parents will continue to feel comfortable having their children taught the tenets of an ostensibly secular faith.

This brings us to the other kind of reform. Those who would bring about a controlled reform from the outside have a dicey problem. They want to use private sector pressure to make the government schools straighten up and fly right, but they don't want this privatization to get completely out of hand. Once parents enjoy a real taste of educational freedom, the result might be that the government schools would clean up their act—but they would still lag behind the free schools. This would mean that no one would return to them, and they would eventually fail rather than reform. Partial privatization is difficult to do. It is like leaving the door to the monkey house partially open.

Nevertheless, partial privatization is still being attempted. A widespread acceptance of vouchers would create a host of quasi-public schools. In other words, these schools would be free (for the time being) of some of the more burdensome regulations that keep traditional government schools from educating their charges. But if they began to get "too free," they could be quickly reminded that their survival as a school next year would be dependent on receiving government vouchers. The idea is to introduce the oxymoronic reform of controlled freedom.

Our current system of government education is socialistic. The government owns and controls the means of educational production. If this were done with the production of steel, for example, we would call it socialism. But many of the education reforms are actually moving us toward fascism. Fascism as an economic system occurs when the government does not "own" the means of production but to a large measure controls them. Private ownership is still allowed but in this case does not mean what it used to mean.

Economically speaking, all voucher proposals are the first step in instituting economic fascism in education—private ownership and public control. As I wrote in *The Paideia of God*, vouchers "will simply change the nature of our educational slavery; they will not usher in educational liberty. Instead of the educational socialism we have now, we will have educational fascism."[4]

But the pressure for vouchers remains strong. "Today 37 states and the District of Columbia have enacted charter school or voucher legislation."[5] Public support for this kind of reforming activity is strong. "Surveys consistently show that the American people are in favor of introducing this competitive element into the world of education."[6] And perhaps a Machiavellian support for vouchers could be advocated—from a distance. In other words, going from freedom to fascism is simply a net loss all around. But going from socialism to fascism might bring about the (unintended) collapse of the established school system and give parents a faint taste of freedom that would make them want more. The fear of that happening appears to underlie the educational establishment's hostility to voucher proposals. They suspect a Trojan horse—and perhaps they are right. Perhaps charter schools and voucher-supported schools will spring up all over the country, and these will prove to be halfway houses, as those addicted to the government's educational money actually break the habit by "tapering off." Maybe. And as a social observer, I might find myself cheering the results.

But in the meantime, private schools that care about their academic integrity need to resolve to have nothing to do with vouchers themselves. He who takes the king's coin becomes the king's man. Whatever kindness God may show to those making their way out of Egypt, those who have already made it out and who have successfully established "unentangled" schools must resolve not to take one step back toward Egypt. There is no good reason for a nonsmoker to start wearing a nicotine patch.

The same principles apply (even more) to charter schools. These schools are completely funded by the government. Depending on the laws, they can eventually become private schools, but as long as they are charter schools, all the basic religious issues remain. They cannot be Christian schools no matter how many Christians might be there teaching in them. Nevertheless, many people are still attracted to this option. It is "no surprise that in the ten years since the first charter law was passed in Minnesota, more than 2,600 charter schools have sprung up in 37 states."[7]

These schools are seen and understood by parents as a hybrid, and this is acceptable to many, particularly for financial reasons. One parent said that private schools were completely inaccessible financially. And consequently "our charter schools are a great hybrid between state and private school."[8] At the same time, such avowed hybridization is something that should arouse more than a few suspicions. Can two walk together except they be agreed (Amos 3:3)? Is it appropriate to plow with an ox and a mule together (2 Cor. 6:14)? What fellowship has Christ with Belial (2 Cor. 6:15)? The applicability of such passages to education can only be denied by Christians if they also deny the essentially *religious* nature of education. And this is difficult to do. We must come to understand, as I expressed in *The Paideia of God*, that "to argue in favor of vouchers [or charter schools] in our context requires that Christians argue for the one thing we must not argue for at this point in our history—the myth of neutrality."[9] If neutrality is not a myth, then there is nothing wrong with charter schools. Of course, if neutrality existed, there would be nothing wrong with the schools we are trying to leave either. But if neutrality is in fact a myth, then we cannot perpetuate it through various charter school proposals and programs.

At the root, the problem with charter schools and vouchers is not difficult to understand. I've written elsewhere that the theological case against such programs should actually be grounded in the prohibition against stealing.[10] When the government taxes us in order to perform the duties assigned to the civil government by God, Christians clearly can have no consistent ethical objection (Rom. 13:1-7). But if the government adopts responsibilities that God never assigned and begins massive redistributions of wealth accordingly, this creates an ethical problem. King Ahab stole Naboth's vineyard. Even though Ahab was the established authority, he could not alter the reality of this theft by calling it something else—zoning alterations or land reform. Parents who want charter schools and vouchers are asking, in effect, for others to pay higher taxes to fund their children's education—and the whole thing becomes simply "food stamps for the brain." A citizenry may be taxed in order to fund those activities that God requires of the civil magistrate, but secularist education is not one of these activities.

We tend to complain about various government intrusions, but we do not recognize that every intrusion is justified on the basis of some constituency somewhere. Someone receives a benefit. If conservative Christian parents join this parade by seeking a piece of the action, we are demonstrating that we do not understand how our nation has drifted into its current idolatrous statism. As I put it elsewhere, "until we learn to fight statism by refusing to accept *benefits*, our hypocrisy will be evident."[11]

But there is another problem. Some of the reformers who want to maintain contact between education and the state are not interested in the money. Rather, they are insecure about their ability to produce an outstanding education on their own. One of the reasons why many do not want to detach completely from the current system is that they are afraid they will be scorned for their lack of educational expertise, certification, or accreditation. I addressed this problem in *Repairing the Ruins*: "We have been told, both directly and subliminally, that state accreditation is to education what the FDA stamp of approval is to food quality, i.e., the guarantee of rigorous scrutiny by knowledgeable experts."[12] But the reason we are having all this debate over education in the first place is that the whole country pretty much agrees that our state-certified and accredited schools are usually pretty poor. Nevertheless, parents still have a deep faith that accreditation means something because it *ought* to mean something. And so they come to inquire about possible enrollment at a private school, and one of their first questions concerns whether or not the school is accredited—even though the reason they have come to apply is that they are thoroughly unhappy with the school they are leaving, which has been accredited for a hundred years.

Excellence is not guaranteed by a piece of paper. Excellence in education is the result of vision, hard work, parental love, and a clear sense of mission. It does not depend upon bureaucratic accreditation. Again quoting *Repairing the Ruins:*

> So what does genuine excellence mean? Prior to any given curriculum choices, it refers first to an attitude—the attitude of the classical mind. We decide, before we begin, that we will *not* tailor our curriculum to suit the student; rather, we educate the student so that he conforms to, and masters, the curriculum. The process of education is larger than we are, and it transcends the generations currently alive.[13]

When parents and teachers are committed to excellence, they are committed to their children's best interests in education. When they are not, it does not matter who certifies the dismal results.

4

THE NATURE OF MAN

ONE OF THE OLDEST questions confronting thinkers and philosophers concerns the nature and origin of evil. For all humanistic thinkers, it is axiomatic that man must be understood as basically good, because *demos*, man, is god. But if mankind is good, we have a problem with the empirical data. Why do people keep behaving the way they do? To appeal to a list much shorter than it *could* be, where do racism, theft, murder, covetousness, lying, and rape come from?

The answer given to this dilemma goes back at least to Socrates. If man is basically good, then he must do evil things because of ignorance. Therefore, the savior for ignorant man must be education. The antidote to ignorance is teaching. But the contrast of Socratic thinking to the Christian faith is striking. In Christian teaching, man is a sinner and rebel, and he must be saved by Jesus Christ. In the humanistic faith, man does evil because he is untaught, and if he were taught more effectively, or with better-funded programs, or more progressive curricula, then the great savior—education—would straighten out all his internal kinks. This assumption about education as savior is pervasive in the modern world. Philosopher David Stove points out that the assumption occurs in a phrase as apparently benign as "racial prejudice." He says we really ought to refer to it as racial antagonism.

> Accordingly, when we call racial antagonism "racial prejudice," we imply that the antagonism depends on some false or irrational belief about the other race. Now this is a distinctly *cheering* thing to imply. For we all know that it is possible for false or irrational beliefs to be corrected. That, after all, is one of the very things that *education* exists for, and which it often achieves. Here, then, is the secret attraction of the phrase "racial prejudice": it cheers us all up, by suggesting—as "racial antagonism," for

example, does *not* suggest—that it is within the power of education to remove racial antagonism.[1]

But modern society does not want to recognize the existence of any problem that does not admit of a human-engineered solution. This solution invariably comes down to some form of education.

The belief in the inherent goodness of man accompanied the beginning of government education in America. Horace Mann, the father of American government education, put the sentiment this way:

> Again I would say, that, whenever a human soul is born into the world, God stands over it, and pronounces the same sublime fiat, 'Let there be light;' and may the time soon come when all human governments shall cooperate with the divine government in carrying this benediction and baptism into fulfillment![2]

In other words, God sees the infant child as "light," and we experience darkness simply because human governments have not been cooperating with the divine government—we have not agreed with this assessment. When we do come to agree with it—by supplying free, universal education—the fulfillment of inherent human goodness will be at hand. It is not possible to reconcile this position with the orthodox position of the Christian church.

Mortimer Adler speaks in a similar way about the nature of the student when he says that "most college students are at heart good boys and girls . . . it is easy to discover that their sophisticated speech masks a kind of natural goodness."[3] If children are naturally good, then we should be able to coax good behavior out of them, and we can all be nice together. "The voice of Nature, therefore, forbids the infliction of annoyance, discomfort, pain, upon a child, while engaged in study."[4] Schoolwork, in a word, should be *fun*. Of course the Christian objection to this dictum does not mean that we should make the classroom as dismal as possible. It is just that in a fallen world with fallen students, annoyance, discomfort, and sometimes even pain are a necessary part of the equation.

Ignorance in a child can come about in various ways. If, as John Locke taught, a child at birth is a *tabula rasa*, a blank slate, then ignorance later on in life is simply the result of teachers and parents refusing to instruct. The child is waiting for information, but no one brings it to him.

But in the humanist view, this ignorance can also be the result of certain passions within the student overwhelming the higher faculties of reason. In other words, the removal of ignorance comes about as older and wiser teachers instruct the young on how to subordinate the passions to reason. Adler again:

> In the light of all we know about man, without the aid of scientific research, it is demonstrably true that man's well-being depends upon the regulation of his emotional life by reason, what the ancients called the discipline and moderation of the passions. This discipline can be accomplished only by the formation of good habits of action and passion, and these good habits are the moral virtues. To whatever extent the school as an educational institution must deal with the emotions of the young, its aim must be the same as that of the church and of the home, namely, the development of moral virtues. There are difficult questions here about the division of responsibility among the cooperating agencies, such as school, church, and home, but there is no unsolved problem about the end which they all must serve. That the cardinal virtues are prudence, justice, temperance, and fortitude is as certain a truth as any theorem on geometry.[5]

Adler argues here that ignorance, which the school and other institutions are called to remove, is the result of passions rising up within the student and blurring what he or she should understand in the light of reason. The standard that Adler appeals to is that of natural moral law. He says that "moral thinking, unlike geometry, does not rest on postulates but commands assent to its conclusions because they are drawn from self-evident first principles—traditionally known as natural moral law."[6]

This approach to the question is ancient, but despite Adler's great gifts, it is still out of step with a more biblical understanding. The Bible does not speak of subordinating the emotions to reason, as the rationalists desire, or even of subordinating reason to the emotions, as the romantics want. Rather, the whole man—body, soul, spirit—should be subordinated to the Word of God. The greatest commandment, given in the context of education, requires that we love God with all our heart, soul, mind, and strength (Deut. 6:4-9). In other words, reason and emotion should stop squabbling like cantankerous siblings and learn to obey their parents directly. Reason must submit to Scripture. The emotions must be brought under the authority of Scripture. And it is the task of true education to see that both do so. Douglas Jones comments on how far we have to go to get there:

> Whatever the exact case, emotion plays a very central role in knowing. Needless to say, this has giant implications for a philosophy of education. Most often, we assume education is just about ideas and information. But if no genuine knowledge can occur without the presence of certain emotions, then moral/emotional education would seem to have to play a much bigger part. But "emotional education" involves far more bodily wisdom and subtlety than a typical curriculum could ever hope to capture.[7]

In the humanistic approach, there are two basic ways for the "savior" to address the problem of ignorance. One is the "straightforward" idea that the task of educators is to fill the student's head with facts. What the student does not know, the teacher will tell him, and, presto, the ignorance is gone. The other approach is the more classical humanist view, which at least has the strength of seeing the whole student and not just a part of him. Here the educator attempts to help the rational side of the student learn to suppress the passionate side. Both approaches exhibit a deep commitment to reason—to reason as a savior. Horace Mann said, "What can *save* us, and our children after us, from eternal, implacable, universal war, but the greatest of all human powers,—the power of impartial thought?"[8]

A third approach might be one advocated by Nietzsche, who would want to actively encourage the subordination of the rational capacities to the "ennobling" passions. I mention Nietzsche because of the regard some have for him, but his view is not really a practical contender in the battles over education. A school in which the students were *encouraged* to let their "ennobling" passions run riot would not last very long before the SWAT teams were called, especially if the educational experiment got way out of hand, as it did before Allied troops began closing in on Berlin.

The Christian faith does not see any aspect of man as trustworthy— neither his reason nor his passions. Humans are fallen, and that fallenness must be taken into account as children are learning to trust in Christ as their Savior and are learning what it means to live in this world while they are growing up into that salvation. People are fallen, but what did they fall from? People have been saved in Christ, but what is that salvation *to*?

This question brings the discussion to a deeper level. Apart from the moral and ethical questions about human behavior, what *is* man? When we consider what man is and what he ought to be, we are also addressing the question of what children are supposed to become. And this requires us to examine what the Scriptures teach about the *imago Dei*, the image of God in human beings.

Every builder should have a blueprint. He should not build in a random or haphazard manner. It is the same with educators. They should have a blueprint. *Where are we going with this?*

Christians understand that our children are created in the image of God, and though sin has marred that image, it is still there. The work of salvation that God has undertaken in this world is to remake all redeemed men and women into a restored image of God. The perfect example of that restored, final image is the new man, the Lord Jesus Christ. We are being built up into Him.

But for the humanists, man is nothing more than the end product of so many years of aimless evolution. Where is this all going? Who knows? As C. S. Lewis noted so ably in his "Evolutionary Hymn," this can be problematic:

> *Lead us, Evolution, lead us*
> *Up the future's endless stair:*
> *Chop us, change us, prod us, weed us.*
> *For stagnation is despair:*
> *Groping, guessing, yet progressing,*
> *Lead us nobody knows where.*[9]

The philosopher Jean-Paul Sartre once said that without an infinite reference point, every finite point is absurd. This statement is exactly correct and explains why every secular classroom is a manifest absurdity. The need for an infinite reference point explains why an understanding that each child bears the image of God is so central to the process of Christian education. Louis Berkhof makes the point profoundly:

> The image of God is the most fundamental thing in humanity generally, and consequently also in the child specifically. And that which is most essential in the child cannot be ignored in its education without doing injustice to both the child and its Creator and without turning its education into perversion.[10]

Berkhof continues by contrasting this Christian view of the child and his education with the necessary implications of an evolutionary view of the child. He shows what happens when Christian parents try to have it both ways—educating a child on the Lord's Day as though he bears God's image, but teaching him throughout the rest of the week as though he does not.

> How can an education that proceeds in part on the assumption that the child is the image-bearer of God and in part on the supposition that it bears the image of the animal, an education that is partly religious and partly irreligious, i.e., anti-religious, ever result in a life that is truly unified? It can only lead to one thing, and that is a divided life so strongly condemned by our Savior (Matt. 6:22, 23), a life with scattered energies and dissipated powers, swayed and torn by conflicting opinions, lacking in singleness of purpose, in stability and strength, and in that true joy that fills the soul which is consciously moving in the right direction.[11]

In order to teach a child rightly, his parents and teachers must know both who and what they are, and they must know this on the authority of God's Word. They must understand that mankind has fallen away from the initial task assigned in the Garden of Eden, but that Jesus Christ came in order to make it possible for people to resume work on that task. Given the nature of the case, men and women must either serve God or refuse to do so. They must either serve God or man. This is the fundamental question before us in all our debates about education.

> Education cannot properly be separated from man's calling in terms of the purpose of God, since he will either be educated for dominion as God's vicegerent, or else for autonomy, and that means in the end the domination of man by man and the subjugation of men not to God and His purpose, but to men and their corrupt desires, and even to creation itself.[12]

If two men were building a house together, but they both held tightly to differing sets of blueprints, it would not be to the point to say that they still had much in common. They both own hammers, saws, nails, carpenter's belts, and so on, and let us say that both of them were of comparable competence. They would soon come to blows if they persisted in trying to build two different houses on the same site. If one wanted a split-level ranch house, and the other wanted a beach bungalow, everything they had in common would be irrelevant. But this is exactly the tension in every secular classroom where Christian children attend. One builder wants to further the process of evolution, and the other wants to develop the image of Jesus Christ in students. The only way to keep the peace is for one of the builders to surrender his blueprints. Thus far, except where Christians have removed their children, the surrendering has been done by the Christians.

> We are not at liberty, as Christians, to subject our children to an education which baptizes them into the godless image of fallen man. Man's humanity consists in his being the bearer of God's image, and it is this image which is of primary importance and the reference point in the child's education at every level.[13]

5

THE CASE AGAINST GOVERNMENT SCHOOLS

DESPITE OUR DIRE educational circumstances, many Christians still believe there is hope for the government school system. Their efforts in trying to restrain the moral corruption of the government schools today have been heroic. While I want to argue for the moral necessity of removing Christian children from these schools, I want to do so with the recognition that Scripture does not list a sin called "sending one's children to public school." These Christians often understand many of the more objectionable aspects of the school system, and they are courageous and diligent in their fight against them.

> Schools still face formidable foes: postmodern secular teaching and liberal agendas, policies that need to change, overly large classes, problems with discipline and the need for higher academic standards. But if, like Nehemiah, we mix prayer with works, if parents are actively and prayerfully involved in their children's education, the evidence shows that public schools can change.[1]

While it is true that faith is an assurance of things hoped for, the evidence of things not seen, I am afraid this confidence that we can "turn things around" remains unduly optimistic. The more glaring symptoms of our disease *can* be ameliorated—but this is not the same thing as a cure. Christian parents who have abdicated responsibility for their children to the government school *are* guilty of sinful negligence. And I am afraid that those godly parents there who are refusing to abdicate, who are fighting the good fight, are expending their energy in a way that I believe could be employed elsewhere with much greater fruitfulness.

I have no desire to be unnecessarily divisive, but I would urge all Christian reformers in the public schools to reconsider their strategic position.

Americans like to get to the bottom line quickly. And so here it is: Given what we have seen to this point, there is no good reason for Christian parents to entrust their children to the government school system. As I wrote in *Standing on the Promises*, "Christian education is not a luxury or an option. It is part of Christian discipleship for those who have been blessed with children."[2] I want to argue that Christian education is a necessity.

The government schools are a central and essential part of the American civil religion, and the remaining commitment to it is largely a matter of "religious" allegiance. If one were to attack waste in a minor part of the Department of Agriculture, and go so far as to argue for the elimination of the entire program, the cheers would be loud in many quarters. But while criticism of the government schools is standard, that criticism does not go so far as to urge the elimination of the schools. In the ancient pagan world, belief in the gods usually died long before a willingness to dispense with the forms of worship. It is the same here. We no longer believe in the gods of education, but our commitment to their temples is still religious and deep. And this is why Christians, who serve another God, must leave *for the right reasons*. They must leave, understanding the antithesis between true religion and idolatry.

> An education that denies God and His Word as the interpretive principle of all things, including all academic disciplines, is an education that implicitly denies the whole of biblical truth and the validity of the Christian faith. To subject our children to such an education is to deny the sovereignty and Lordship of God over our children and thus apostasy from the faith.[3]

We must first remember the history of the government school movement. The beginning of government education in America must be understood as a messianic movement. The common schools were going to be the means by which the entire progressive agenda was ushered in. This was necessary, given the theological commitments of those progressives. As discussed in an earlier chapter, if the Christian faith is not true, and we are not created by God and marred by sin, then the question arises—how do we come to do evil? As we saw, the typical humanist answer is that people do evil *because of ignorance*. And if sin is ignorance, then education is salvation. The various incarnate forms of this "messiah" can and do vary (from Socratic dialectic to bureaucratic certification), but the same basic religious impulse is at work.

At the rise of common schools in America, the thinkers who pushed this agenda were self-consciously rebelling against the dominant Calvinistic ethos established in colonial America. Government education was birthed in a revolutionary rejection of the historic Christian faith, and the progressive claims for the saving power of education were breathtaking.

Christians were misled because of the gradual centralization of the schools. In the beginning, the Unitarians were the movers and shakers of the movement, but school boards were still controlled by local people, and this meant that many of the government schools at their establishment were evangelical and Protestant "on the ground." As the logic of religious education in a broadly pluralistic society worked its way to the surface, the distinctively Christian features of these local schools have gradually been squeezed out. When I was a boy in public school, our days began with prayer. In the earlier days, we also had catechisms in government schools. Now it is hard to find them in *churches*. In schools the prayers were the last to go.

But many Christians still think of local government schools as being somehow "our" schools. Because local government was significant at the founding of our nation, and because many of the *forms* of local government have been kept intact, many Christians still think this is the case. So when the Supreme Court has something to say about prayers at high school football games, many Americans still think of this as an odd or strange intrusion—that can somehow be reversed— as opposed to the logical outworking of the very idea of the government school system. And thus it is that we tend to focus our desire for reform on how the schools *look*, instead of thinking about what they *are*. But this tendency merely obscures the real issue, as I show in *Repairing the Ruins*:

Why prayer in an officially agnostic institution? Why the teaching of creation in an officially pluralistic institution? Why do we think it is a victory when the pagans admit our Lord, as an option just for some, to their pantheon of gods many and lords many?[4]

Still, in recent years many Christians have (finally) become disillusioned and have been leaving the government schools in ever increasing numbers. This trend is better than nothing and appears to be the beginning of true repentance, but such reaction often places the alternative forms of education that then develop on the wrong reactionary footing. Christians should *act* in obedience to the Word, not *react* to the various forms of disobedience around them. Reaction to problems in the government school system is not the same thing as having a biblical theology of education.

Of course, the things parents tend to react to *are* certainly to be avoided. But mere "avoidance," because it is not grounded on obedience to the Scriptures, does not successfully avoid *all* the sin that displeases God. In the best case scenario, such reaction is little better than getting out of the fire and into the frying pan. The bright side is that such reactions sometimes make parents realize that they do not really have a theology of children and education, and this pushes them back into the Scriptures. And some of these attention-getters are becoming harder and harder to ignore—they just won't get off the front page of the newspaper.

Danger: It is not uncommon now for kids to have to go through metal detectors in order to get to class. Some schools have an uncanny resemblance to a minimum security prison. What parent would want going to school to somehow merit the Bronze Star? This point does not need belaboring.

Academic incompetence: In addition, all the trouble and danger are not worth it. It would be one thing to risk danger to recover a treasure, such as fistfuls of diamonds. But who would risk his life for a handful of driveway gravel? Paul Simon put it well, and perhaps far better than he knew: "When I think back on all the crap I learned in high school, it's a wonder I can think at all."

But even here, the issues are worldview matters. We do not understand that our academic slide has occurred *because it had to*. We cannot reject the tree and continue to demand the fruit. The universe coheres because Christ is Lord—and there is no alternative center, no other *arche* on standby in case He fails. Nonbelievers can teach the truth in any given area only on the basis of common grace—that is, if they borrow Christian categories on the sly in order to do so. But when nonbelievers grow increasingly aware of their epistemological assumptions, they begin rejecting the very concept of truth—every manifestation of it—and they embrace the absurd. And this is why the *only* place where academic integrity can flourish over time is in a Christian school.

> The ground for the necessity of Christian schools lies in this very thing, that no fact can be known unless it be known in its relationship to God. And once this point is clearly seen, the doubt as to the value of teaching arithmetic in Christian schools falls out of the picture. Of course arithmetic must be taught in a Christian school. It cannot be taught anywhere else.[5]

Immorality: Sexual immorality in the government schools is rampant and expected. Drugs are common. Drinking and drunkenness are standard fare. Worse than this, many forms of the immorality are even *encouraged* in grotesque sex education classes. But as stated earlier, a parent can recognize all these things and pull a child away from them and still not know the *nature* of a parent's duty in education.

Mere reaction is not good enough. Believing parents must come to see Christian education as a demand of the covenant. Children of Christian parents belong to God. They are His by virtue of the covenant God made with His people. The prophet Ezekiel charges the people of Israel with great sin because they sacrificed their children to idols. But God's anger is directed at them because of the identity of the children— they were children "whom they bare unto me" (Ezek. 23:37). God calls their children *His* children. They were children of the covenant, and they belonged to God. In both old covenant and new, God requires that His children be brought up in a certain way.

As I pointed out elsewhere, "Christian parents are morally obligated to keep their children out of government schools because the Scriptures expressly require a non-agnostic form of education."[6] More directly, God requires that covenant children be brought up in covenant truths.

In the law, God gives His greatest commandment, and He does so in the midst of His requirements for the education of His children:

> *Hear, O Israel: The* LORD *our God is one* LORD: *And thou shalt love the* LORD *thy God with all thine heart, and with all thy soul, and with all thy might. And these words, which I command thee this day, shall be in thine heart: And thou shalt teach them diligently unto thy children, and shalt talk of them when thou sittest in thine house, and when thou walkest by the way, and when thou liest down, and when thou risest up. And thou shalt bind them for a sign upon thine hand, and they shall be as frontlets between thine eyes. And thou shalt write them upon the posts of thy house, and on thy gates. (Deut. 6:4-9)*

In the Psalms we see the importance of covenant education as well. When that education fails, the terms of the covenant are not kept over the course of generations.

> *For he established a testimony in Jacob, and appointed a law in Israel, which he commanded our fathers, that they should make them known to their children: That the generation to come might know them, even the children which should be born; who should arise and declare them to their children: That they might set their hope in God, and not forget the works of God, but keep his commandments: And might not be as their fathers, a stubborn and rebellious generation; a generation that set not their heart aright, and whose spirit was not steadfast with God. (Ps. 78:5-8)*

In these passages we see the *comprehensiveness* of what God requires. When you walk along the road. When you lie down. When you rise up. All the law and all the testimony is to be taught to the next generation. Because God has given such requirements, there is no middle ground. "All of life is under the authority of God's revealed Word, and children were to be taught in terms of this comprehensive authority *all the time*."[7]

Stephen Perks makes the point well: "Either we educate our children in terms of a Christian culture, or we hand them over to be educated by humanists as pagans. Our actions in this matter will help to determine and shape the culture of the next generation."[8]

The New Testament does not rescind this obligation at all. "And, ye fathers, provoke not your children to wrath: but bring them up in the nurture and admonition of the Lord" (Eph. 6:4). The grounds for leaving the government schools is grounded on Scripture and not on simple reaction. As I wrote in *Excused Absence*, "The obligation of Christians to provide a Christian education for their children is one that existed in Scripture long before prayer and the Ten Commandments were driven out of government schools."[9]

We may order our lives in accordance with the Word of God or on the basis of the word of man. These two positions are necessarily and fundamentally at odds.

> These two positions are mutually exclusive. They can never agree fundamentally on the interpretation of the facts of reality at any point if they are consistent with their presuppositions. For the Christian and the humanist, therefore, there can be no common ground. This truth has been understood more by the humanists heretofore than it has by the Christians. It is the mutual exclusiveness of these two positions which makes the provision of a specifically Christian education for our children essential, and the sending of our children to state schools to be educated by humanists a denial of the faith implicitly.[10]

Despite such plain injunctions, one of the most common arguments in favor of sending Christian children to the government schools is what might be called the "salt and light" argument. Our children are having a good influence there—maybe not on the institution as a whole, but they still have an evangelistic presence. A few quick answers. First, the argument is not true. The unbelievers are having a far more profound impact on our children than our children have on them. Secondly, evangelism is not a duty to be undertaken without training and teaching. Parents use this as a reason, but they acknowledge the need for preparation to be salt and light in other settings. Who sends their kids to Vacation Bible Schools run by the Mormons in order that they might be salt and light? Who sends their eight-year-old to India to be a missionary? The reason they do not is because training, preparation, and *education* are necessary in order to be salt and light. *Preparation is necessary.*

Other parents settle for a good deal less. They point to the (indisputable) evidence that some Christian kids survive their experience in the government schools. This is quite true, but it is also a perverse argument. People survive plane crashes, too, and cancer. This is not an *argument* for them. There is no point to playing a game when all you are going to do is play defense. The Scriptures tell us that our duty is to bring every thought captive to Jesus Christ (2 Cor. 10:4). If we want to do this in the government schools, if we play offense, then we are saying we want to make them Christian schools, and this would lead to another debate on another issue—the propriety of tax-funded Christian schools. And these could possibly be defended provided the government funding the schools was also Christian. But until then, to receive government funding is a way of subordinating the authority of Christ to the authority of Caesar. If we do not want conquest, then what *are* we doing there?

Of course, this raises the question of teaching in these schools. The problems attending this issue are very different from the problems of sending kids there. The kids are "worldview-defenseless." An adult need not be. But the adult's problem is different. *If* the teacher is clueless (like the third grader is), he or she should be doing something else other than teaching. If the person is not clueless, then he or she is either going to be constantly exasperated—or fired. If the teacher fails to reach those around him, he or she will be exasperated. If the teacher succeeds, he or she will be fired. All in all, those gifted in teaching should seek out classical Christian academies in which to teach—even if salary and retirement benefits are lower.

One way or another, Christians should get out. But again, it is important to get out for the right reasons. Otherwise, we will simply duplicate the errors of the government schools in the institutions we eventually build. And who wants that?

The stakes are indeed high. How long will Christian parents continue to assume that they can sow one thing in the education of their children and reap another in the lives of these children once grown?

And can Christian parents reasonably expect their children to be imbued with a spirit of true religion if they persist in sending them to a school where for twenty-four hours a week they are taught in a spirit that is fundamentally irreligious, if not positively anti-Christian? The answer can only be a decided negative. And experience will bear out the correctness of this answer. America is today reaping in its churches what it has sown in its schools. It has sown through the secularized schools, and it is reaping a purely naturalistic religion.[11]

This concern is far greater than a simple concern over how these children will come to live throughout the course of their individual lives, although that is obviously part of it. Because education is a cultural issue, a threat in the realm of education is a threat to the broader culture as well. And we have only two alternatives—will the culture reflect the standards of God's Word, or will it not?

> It is through the education of our children that our worldview is passed on to future generations and our civilization thereby preserved. Christians, therefore, have a very simple choice: either they educate their children in terms of godly learning and discipline and a Christian world-view, a covenantal, dominion-oriented worldview, and thereby help to build and preserve Christian civilization, or they hand over the education of their children to pagans who will educate them in terms of ungodly learning and discipline and a pagan worldview, and thereby help to build a pagan civilization which will enslave their children to the world they are called to rule over.[12]

But when we first learn of this antithesis, it is still too easy to simply turn away from ungodly culture with fear and loathing. Indeed we should turn away, but that is only a small part of our responsibility. Our God keeps covenant, Scripture says, to a thousand generations, and we must understand that curses and blessings are both part of the covenant. God promises curses for those covenant members who hate Him and serve idols. The prospect of a curse by itself (although it is quite true) can create the wrong kind of fear. We know that perfect love casts out fear, because fear has to do with punishment. At the same time, we are told to work out our salvation with fear and *trembling*. When we understand this rightly, the thing that should make us tremble is the height and depth and breadth of God's *grace*. Educated under the wrong kind of fear, our children will become servile in their thinking. Educated under no fear of God at all, they will become arrogant. And so applying all this to the subject of education, God demands that we teach our children (*His* children) in accordance with their station. They are royalty and should receive a royal education. The mark of such an education is confident humility.

> Now, the children of the covenant are adopted into a family that is infinitely higher than the family of any man of rank or nobility. . . . Should we not bend all our efforts to make it [their education] richer and fuller, and to bring it more into harmony with their high calling and

exalted duties? Would we want our children to be a dishonor to the household of God? Let us ever be mindful of the fact that the King's children must have a royal education.[13]

Lesslie Newbigin puts the point well: "Is it or is it not the case that every human being exists for the joy of eternal fellowship with God and must face the possibility of missing that mark, forfeiting that prize? If it is the case, it ought to be part of the core curriculum in every school."[14]

6

THE CENTRALITY OF WORSHIP

WE MUST BEGIN WITH a somewhat complicated or paradoxical observation. We cannot confine to the classroom the view that teaching cannot be confined to the classroom. In other words, it is pointless to talk about how the Christian worldview embraces all of life and then only talk about it in the classroom. We easily slip into the error of thinking that education is a question of mere data transfer, of getting sentences from older, grayer heads into younger, tousled heads. But Christian education is not mere data transfer. And even though it is tempting for some Christians to taunt the government schools over their failures in this regard, we have to recognize that this is not a battle between our successful data transfers and their unsuccessful ones. And this means we must learn the centrality of worship.

Worship is central to life; therefore, it is central to education for that life. The ancient Greek notion is that mankind should be defined and understood as *homo sapiens*, with humans defined by their ability to think. But in the Christian view, man is *homo adorans*, worshiping man. What men and women are in the presence of God defines them; in the light of this, they learn to think, love, walk, emote, and sing in a certain way. Jim Jordan makes this point well:

> The second reason why Christian education has not fulfilled its promise is that modern evangelical Christians do not understand what human beings are. Human beings are not, as the Greco-Roman tradition teaches, *homo sapiens*, "thinking man." Rather, we are *homo adorans*, "worshiping man," something the Bible teaches and which the older pagans had not yet forgotten. Sadly, the Greek assumption seems to underlie most Christian education.[1]

A Christian worldview is not a matter of having an opinion about everything, with all those opinions being interconnected or, as some might say, entangled. Our lives are supposed to go together *a certain way*. Parents who have labored over assembling a child's Christmas present, one with multiple parts, know that it is not sufficient to throw all the parts together into a box and call it a tricycle. Neither is it adequate to throw all our opinions into a box and call it a worldview.

But in order for our lives to cohere rightly, in order for the parts to go together in that certain way, the point of integration cannot be down here "under the sun." Solomon taught us that under the sun everything is vanity. He taught us the only way for the fragments of this vain world to come together. Only God can draw straight with crooked lines.

Before I address the importance of worship in education, the sorry state of our broader Christian culture requires a few disclaimers. Worship is not the same thing as praise. Praise is an important part of worship, but the two words are not synonyms. But, through an unhappy turn of phrase, the music portion of the worship service is referred to by many as the "worship time." Nor is worship about getting our felt needs stroked. The posture of the worshiper in Scripture is to kneel or lie prostrate. For many moderns a worship service should be a cozy place. But for sinners, even justified sinners, true worship is anything but comfortable. It is unfortunate indeed that Rat and Mole had a greater sense of the numinous in the presence of the god Pan than many modern evangelicals do in the presence of the God of Abraham. And worship is not a retreat from the world. Rather, worship opens heaven to us in such a way that the earth comes into focus. And this is why worship is relevant to education in the classroom.

True worship is incarnational. If we want to understand how transcendence and immanence intersect, we have to come to understand these things in Christ. And we cannot understand the incarnation of Christ by sitting in neat rows in a classroom, doing push-ups with the brain. We have to have water applied to us in the triune name; we have to hear the Gospel preached and learn practical obedience to the Word declared; and we have to take and eat. In short, we have to learn how to worship. And then, having worshiped, we are sent out into the world to study it, subdue it, replenish it. But education and learning follow worship and proceed from it.

Jesus Christ is the *arche*, the One in whom all things hold together (Col. 1:18). But *Christ* is not a mere word we use; Jesus Christ is the Son of God, seated at the right hand of God the Father. There is no Christian worldview where He is not present. And He has determined the conditions under which He is covenantally present. Someone might object and say that God is omnipresent. This is quite true, but there is a difference between God's presence as Creator and His presence in the worship service of His own people as their covenantal Redeemer, with blessing or cursing in plain view.

Every society has institutions that are respected and honored. On the creaturely level, such institutions may be considered sacred, or having sanctity, so long as we use the lower case *s*. As Christians, we think of such examples as the sanctity of life or the sacredness of marriage. But we know that only God is ultimately holy. We say that a human institution is sacred in the same way that we might argue that a poet or artist is creative. We know the whole time that only God creates and that we as creatures cannot create *ex nihilo* as God can. Nevertheless, we bear the image of God, and we can mimic His creativity and approximate it. But unless He had created, we would have nothing to mimic, and, to add insult to injury, we wouldn't exist either.

In the same way, institutions worthy of respect and honor derive their respectability from that which is ultimately sacred. The Bible teaches us that creaturely holiness is derivative and that we are to be holy because He is holy (1 Pet. 1:16). All sanctity in Israel derived from the Holy of Holies. This is why respect for any human institution depends upon what that society considers to be ultimately holy. And this is why all attempts at educational reformation will fail apart from reformation of worship. If we will not honor the center, then why on earth would we care to honor the periphery?

Education that does not begin and end in heaven is not true education. Our salvation began before the foundation of the world in the purposes of God. We trust in Christ and seek eternal life through faith in Him. But in the meantime, our only access to heaven is through worship. And so put simply, a Christian school will not succeed in teaching children to think and live as Christians unless these young people are "going to heaven" once a week on the Lord's Day. Further, they must know that they do so.

> The Christian school, then, must be viewed as serving *in loco parentis* and in *loco ecclesiae*. It is not "either/or." It's "both/and." If the chief end of Christian education is to train up worshipers, then Christian education must be seen as the duty of the Church. It is certainly not the duty of elders to carry out every detail of that education, but they are responsible for the oversight of it. It is the duty of elders to be fathers of fathers.[2]

This is why a classical Christian school will not succeed in its mission unless it has the strong support of a worshiping community. Sometimes a school has been planted first, but one of the first things to become obvious to the parents and teachers is the need for a supportive church or churches.

There are some "practical" reasons why, obviously. A good church understands discipline, and the people who worship there understand it as well. If they enroll their children in a school that practices discipline, they won't be shocked or dismayed by it. In a similar way, a healthy church understands and declares that all religious claims are total. When the school applies Christian worldview thinking to subjects such as grammar or mathematics, this is seen as an application of what is preached on the Lord's Day. But if a school is patronized by Christians from churches that teach that God's Word has limited applications and that there is such a thing as academic neutrality, the worldview teaching at the school will become controversial.

But the major reason why worship is central concerns the children. Worship is the point of integration for all Christian living, including the living that goes on at the school. When children who are members of the race *homo adorans* worship God rightly, everything comes together in their lives. When they do not, everything is out of joint. When a school is filled with students whose lives are out of joint, not to mention the lives of their parents and teachers, there is no way the endeavor can be blessed.

7

WHAT IS EDUCATION?

As MENTIONED IN the last chapter, religious claims are always total—all-encompassing. If Christ is not the Lord of all, then He is not the Lord at all. To claim that a particular religious dogma is not total is tantamount to the claim that it is not really religious. In short, such limitations are always a denial of the faith in principle, and they make room for another claim from another faith. This other claim is truly religious, and can be identified as such because the claim is total.

Unfortunately, many Christian schools embrace this faulty line of thinking. They see our pluralistic society as a great tossed salad, and they are simply one small evangelical crouton. Discussion of a Christian worldview application is heard by them—regularly—within the limited context of that crouton. Consistent Christianity is, for them, limited to what goes on within the walls of the school and is not seen as encompassing all of life, for which life the training in the school is supposed to be preparation. Although they would never state it so baldly, they appear to have quietly translated the Great Commission into something like, "Therefore go unto all nations, and do your best to fit right in, supplementing their perspective with your perspective."

But a consistent Christian pedagogy sees education as inherently religious, as something that involves the whole person in the context of the whole universe, a universe created by the triune God. R. L. Dabney addresses this topic with characteristic clarity: "Education is the nurture and development of the whole man for his proper end. That end must be conceived rightly in order to understand the process, and even man's earthly end is predominantly moral."[1]

When Dabney says that man's end is moral, he does not mean that it is *moralistic*. That is, a child cannot be educated simply through being given a list of do's and don'ts. Rather, man's end is related to the glory of God, as the catechism says, and whether or not he will live under the blessing of God is determined by that moral relation. Obedience in education is the process of learning the implications of that moral relation as it relates to every aspect of our lives.

Berkhof and Van Til summarize the Christian understanding of education quite properly:

> But what, then, do we mean by education? *Education is implication into God's interpretation.* No narrow intellectualism is implied in this definition. To think God's thoughts after him, to dedicate the universe to its Maker, and to be the vicegerent of the Ruler of all things: this is man's task. Man is prophet, priest, and king. It is this view of education that is involved in and demanded by the idea of creation.[2]

A human being sitting in a classroom has not achieved his highest good. Christian education is not a rationalistic exercise. A student who learns various points of Christian doctrine and who reproduces his understanding successfully on the pages of a test, but who then goes out and lives the same way the students across town at the government school do, represents a failure in Christian education. If everything is to be understood as integrated in Christ—whether biology, history, math, science, Latin, or rhetoric—then surely we are to understand Christ as the integration point between the lessons of the classroom and the rest of life.

> For the Christian the purpose of education is to facilitate maturation in the image of God and thus growth into true manhood and womanhood, so that the child might be able to fulfill his creation mandate in obedience to God's word. It follows from this that the kind of education we give our children must be one which is thoroughly grounded in the Christian worldview and which seeks to subject every discipline to the authority of God's word as it is revealed in the Scriptures of the Old and New Testaments. Education is thus inescapably a covenant activity; indeed it is a central aspect of man's covenant duty. Hence to deny our children such an education is to abandon our responsibilities as the covenant people of God.[3]

The Scriptures are to be practically authoritative in the classroom so that the students might see in microcosm how the Scriptures are authoritative everywhere else. They are not authoritative in that classroom as a substitute for obedience elsewhere.

The authority of the Scriptures is seen in the direction of the education, the purpose of it, the rationale for it, and the foundation of it. But that authority is not established by opening with a prayer and sprinkling a few pious phrases on the math worksheets.

> Sometimes some say sneeringly, or at least doubtfully, "How can you be specifically Christian when you teach the children that two times two are four?" Well, our answer is that if you cannot teach arithmetic to the glory of God, you cannot do it any other way because it cannot be done any other way by anybody. And by this I do not mean that you have breathed a sort of Christian atmosphere about the problems of arithmetic in the sense that you have opened the school session with prayer a couple hours before. By a Christian atmosphere I mean first of all that deep conviction on the part of the teacher that no fact is teachable except when brought into relationship with God.[4]

God is our life. In Him we live and move and have our being. If He had not created the world, we would not be here (and hence could not do our math). If He had not created the world, there would be no oranges, and hence we could not discover that two oranges plus two oranges make four of them. The fact that the Scriptures are at the center of all Christian education does not mean that the students and teacher walk around the classroom two inches above the floor with a strange luminosity surrounding their heads. It means that the students are learning how to present their bodies, brains and all, math puzzles in them and everything, as living sacrifices, holy and acceptable to God. Such an approach to education is surprisingly earthy, and yet the earthiness is not pointless, as it is in a secularist context. Van Til says, "Christian teachers know that not a single 'fact' can really be known and therefore really be taught unless placed under the light of the revelation of God."[5]

All secular approaches to education are bound by time and space, or, to use Solomon's phrase, they pursue their futilities "under the sun." They may attempt the creation of pseudo-transcendentals (false absolutes—idols of the mind) by appealing to the ancient world as classicists do, or to ideas as the philosophers do, or to the state as the collectivists do, or to the individual as the libertarians do. But nothing coheres, nothing obeys, nothing *tastes*.

In contrast, Mortimer Adler sees the task of education as one of preparing the student to participate in the great conversation that has occurred down through the ages. "We have often described the great books as enacting a great conversation through the ages—a conversation about the basic ideas, the fundamental problems, the major subject matters which concern the mind and heart of man."[6] When the process is done, the student is erudite and informed. "The direct product of liberal education is a good mind, well disciplined in its processes of inquiring and judging, knowing and understanding, and well furnished with knowledge, well cultivated by ideas."[7] This is good, but there are still limits. Those who have participated in "great books" conversations inspired by this approach to modern classicism know that few things can wreck the intellectual party more quickly than a claim of absolute truth, goodness, or beauty. The student is equipped for anything the great conversation might bring to him, except for one thing—answers. To travel hopefully is better than to arrive.

A conversation in C. S. Lewis's *Great Divorce* illustrates well two contrary views on the *point* of intellectual activity.

> "But you must feel yourself that there is something stifling about the idea of finality? Stagnation, my dear boy, what is more soul-destroying than stagnation?"
>
> "You think that because hitherto you have experienced truth only with the abstract intellect. I will bring you where you can taste it like honey and be embraced by it as by a bridegroom. Your thirst shall be quenched."[8]

The Christian faith claims that in Jesus Christ all things find their only possible coherence. This faith is therefore inescapably imperialistic and cannot retain its integrity if it is made over into anything else. This "imperialism" is not only present in education but is present in everything, and it must be explicitly and clearly taught. For education is the place where we are to teach. As Van Til notes:

> We have resources of principles such as no other commonwealth of education has. More than that. We not only claim our rightful place among

the commonwealths of education, but we have a definitely imperialistic program. No mere Monroe Doctrine will suffice. We are out to destroy—albeit with spiritual weapons only and always—all our competitors. We do not recognize them as equals but regard them as usurpers. Carthage must be destroyed.[9]

The fact that such language scares us indicates how compromised we have allowed ourselves to become. Van Til is not urging the physical destruction of non-Christians—note his "spiritual weapons only and always"—but he does see the task of the Christian educator as one of constant, total war. Every thought must be made captive to Christ. A Christian school is not the place where we complete this task, but it is the place where we teach our children that spiritual warfare *is* the task. As always this instruction is related to a proper understanding of the identity of our children.

> The covenant child belongs to a distinctive, chosen people, a people that is separated from the world in consecration to God. . . . The life of the covenant child should ever increasingly become a true inflection of the life of Christ that is born within the heart. Nothing short of the perfect life is its grand ideal.[10]

As Christian children are given a thoroughly and distinctively Christian education, they will understand the world God placed them in, and they will understand their appointed role in it. They will learn to grow in their sanctification, whether intellectual, ethical, or aesthetic. Moreover, they will also come to understand the futility of what passes for education elsewhere. This understanding will not make them supercilious or proud, but rather will fill them with compassion.

R. V. Young notes the connection between Christian education and evangelism: "The study of Christian culture is necessary in order to restore a sense of genuine reality in the face of the surrealistic landscape of postmodern delusion, and to provide a matrix in which the work of evangelization can take place."[11] Rightly understood, this is the true "salt and light" argument. Before we can win the children of this world, we have to stop losing our children to that world. And as we teach them their identity in Christ in such a way that they embrace that identity and the terms of the covenant that define it, they will provide the kind of contrast with our postmodern culture's lost children that will make evange-lism truly potent. Before we can invite nonbelievers to participate in our believing culture, we have to *have* one. And in order to have one, we have to pass the faith on to our children in spirit and in truth. There are many aspects to this task, but Christian education is right at the center of it.

> Christian education is one of the means which God is pleased to use for working faith into the heart of the child, for calling an incipient faith into action, and for guiding the first faltering steps of faith. It teaches the child to flee from sin and to strive after holiness, without which no one will see the Lord.[12]

8

DEMOCRACY AND EGALITARIANISM

WE SAW IN THE second chapter that the impetus behind the formation of the government schools was democratic and egalitarian, beginning in earnest in the early part of the nineteenth century. This democratic impulse influenced every sector of American life—church, state, and family. After two hundred years of this democratic "tradition," we have a good explanation as to why one of the common objections to classical and Christians schools is that they foster "elitism." Classical educators have to walk a razor edge in representing their schools to outsiders— "striving for excellence" is acceptable—in order to honor the well-established democratic sensibilities. If the brochures they print are not to be a PR nightmare, schools have to kowtow a little.

Every culture has blasphemy laws. They are not always *called* that, but no society allows citizens to rail against the reigning deity. In our pluralistic times, these blasphemy laws are called "hate crimes" legislation, among other euphemisms, but they are really religious protections to keep the reigning god, *demos*, from being blasphemed.

But the Christian faith teaches that God has established the world in hierarchal strata. In contrast, the democratic faith teaches that we are all equal and that any child can become president. In Christian cultures, envy is understood to be one of the seven deadly sins, what Shakespeare identified as a "universal wolf." But in democratic societies, envy is institutionalized, and the tenets of such envy are diligently taught to the democratic young when they rise up, when they lie down, or when they walk along the road. The envy is not called that, of course, but rather goes by names such as fairness, justice, or equality. Such teaching has the effect of discouraging anyone who would establish a school that honors the differences built into the world by God—differences of sex, ability, and so forth. "The modern child is told that he can be anything that he wants to be. The medieval child would have been instructed on how to occupy his station. A moment's reflection should tell us which child is being told the lie."[1]

Schools that effectively teach children to live as Christians (in all humility) will be schools that are accused of encouraging arrogance. Teaching children to be consumed with self is thought of as inculcating a good self-image, and teaching children to honor others is defined as prideful. Isaiah rightly pronounced a woe on those who called evil good and good evil (Isa. 5:20). For example, we have gotten to the point where a preacher can spend the entire sermon talking about himself and his own struggles, and everyone says that he is being open, honest, transparent, and humble. Another man, who proclaims the truth in a way that indicates something would have been true had *he* never been born, is dismissed as an arrogant man. Our categories have gotten inverted, and this is due to the democratic enforcement of the leveling power of envy.

Of course, the problem is exacerbated by the fact that there *are* schools that do cultivate a snobbish, elitist environment. Far from teaching children to learn the nature of the world and how to occupy an appropriate station in it, they are what my daughter Rachel helpfully called classical schools for "show poodles." These schools make it easy for critics who oppose a truly superior *Christian* education (which necessarily includes the inculcation of humility) to dismiss Christian schools as just more prep-school snobbery. According to C. S. Lewis, the democratic spirit, in this diabolical sense, "leads to a nation without great men, a nation mainly of subliterates, full of the cocksureness which flattery breeds on ignorance, and quick to snarl or whimper at the first hint of criticism."[2]

There are two antithetical reasons why people might want to bring an education to every child. The first is Christian kindness. Jesus Christ commanded that the Gospel be preached to every creature, and the foundational records of this Gospel are found in Scripture. We teach people to read so that they might have access to the unmerited kindness of God. Education helps bring this grace to every person. But the second reason is democratic, and it is resentful, not grateful. Justice must be brought to every person—all people have a *right* to an education, and it is robbery to deprive them of it. This language of rights is extremely problematic for those who think in Christian categories. However problematic the language might be, it can be extremely florid. For example, Horace Mann put it this way: "Each parent feels that a free education is as secure a part of the birthright of his offspring as Heaven's bounties of light and air."[3] In other words, for someone to go without an education is like being deprived of sunshine or oxygen.

There is a vast difference between the way Christians and humanists define "civil rights." For a Christian rights tend to be negatively defined. For a humanist they are positively stated. For example, a Christian approach can be seen in such common law rights as the right to trial by jury or *habeas corpus*. A humanist tends to define rights in terms of "affordable housing" or a "living wage." But notice the sleight of hand. The right of one person to a living wage is a demand placed upon another person to pay it, and the assumed right of an intrusive government to enforce it. This means that a right to a free education for all translates to the demand that everyone be forced to pay through the nose for that free education. When Christians insist that *habeas corpus* should be honored in our civil law, they do not impose on anyone other than potential oppressors.

But notice the language of Mann again:

> For these ends, they enjoin upon us a more earnest, a more universal, a more religious devotion of our exertions and resources to the culture of the youthful mind and heart of the nation. Their gathered voices assert the eternal truth, that, IN A REPUBLIC, IGNORANCE IS A CRIME; AND THAT PRIVATE IMMORALITY IS NOT LESS AN OPPROBRIUM TO THE STATE THAN IT IS GUILT IN THE PERPETRATOR.[4]

In other words, everything that everybody does is the state's business. And if any fail to meet the grade, their ignorance is a crime against the republic, and, being such, the republic has the right to defend itself. Universal and mandatory education is therefore necessary in order for democracy as democracy to survive. Not only is universal, mandatory education a "reform" in itself, but for Mann it is the mother of all democratic reforms. "But, in universal education, every 'follower of God and friend of human kind' will find the only sure means of carrying forward

that particular reform to which he is devoted."[5] And for Mann, education *must* be universal.[6]

With this understanding, note what follows from these educational
demands:

> I believe in the existence of a great, immortal, immutable principle of
> natural law, or natural ethics,—a principle antecedent to all human insti-
> tutions, and incapable of being abrogated by any ordinance of man. . . .
> The will of God, as conspicuously manifested in the order of Nature,
> and in the relations which he has established among men, founds the
> *right* of every child that is born into the world, to such a degree of edu-
> cation as will enable him, and, as far as possible, will predispose him, to
> perform all domestic, social, civil, and moral duties, upon the same clear
> ground of natural law and equity as it founds a child's *right*, upon his first
> coming into the world, to distend his lungs with a portion of the com-
> mon air.[7]

To deprive a newborn of air is to murder him. The state has the right,
according to biblical law, to prevent such murder. But if failure to provide fully funded schools is tantamount to such murder, then the power
of the state is greatly increased. In the first case, the government (rightly)
prohibits the murderous taking of life. But in the second, the government has surreptitiously received a mandate to tax everyone throughout
the course of their lives in order to fund the schools for the children—
it being equivalent to murder not to do so.

Government schools will not disappear, therefore, until the democratic assumptions undergirding them disappear. The two go together,
as Adler understood: "in a rightly conceived industrial democracy, liberal education *should be* and *can be* for all men. It should be because they
are all equal as persons, as citizens, from a democratic point of view."[8]

But notice the language of envy in simple statements about college
education: "It is undoubtedly easier to think soundly about liberal education if you are preparing to give it only to the few who are favored in
natural endowments or economic position. But democracy is right, and
we must solve the problem of giving to everyone the sort of college education that is most readily given to the favored few."[9]

"Favored in natural endowments or economic position." "The
favored few." We cannot have that, and so we wind up levying heavy taxes

on the favored few, whose numbers steadily increase until it includes virtually every taxpayer. Then we discover that there is no such thing as a free lunch, which we would have known earlier if these government schools had had classes in basic economics.

In the world created by God, inequities are not removable. Some students will do well, and others will not. Some parents can afford a better school, and others cannot. Some students are smart *and* good-looking, and some of them are athletic to boot. The French Revolution wanted to declare liberty, equality, and fraternity to be in close harmony. In actual fact, when liberty is granted, the first thing to disappear is equality of station. And if equality is mandated, then it will be at the cost of liberty.

The ultimate reason why the democratic impulse is so strong—why we resist such differences—is that the sinful heart resents the final discrimination made in the judgment of God when He separates the sheep from the goats. Spelling tests smack of the Last Day. The way we manage our schools shows how, deep down, we would really like to abolish the Great White Throne Judgment. This resistance extends from the democratic government school system down to the most trivial awards ceremony. And judging from our awards ceremonies, many modern educators do not want God to separate the sheep from the goats. They want Him to hand out participant ribbons to all.

TEN YEARS
AFTER

9

WHAT IS CLASSICAL EDUCATION?

THE RESURGENCE OF classical education over the last decade has been heartening in many respects, but some aspects of it are a bit confusing. No one holds the copyright on the word *classical*, and given the nature of the word, there has been something of a scramble in the various manifestations of classical education. This is not surprising, especially in a time when *classical* can refer to a '57 Chevy, an original cola formula, the early Beach Boys, or a classic rock radio station.

Within the field of education, the word *classical* has a number of legitimate applications and a few spurious ones. There is the democratic classicism promoted by Mortimer Adler. There is the elite classicism of the well-established wealthy prep schools. We also see the classical approach advocated by David Hicks, which has been called "moral classicism." And then there is the classicism argued for in these pages and practiced in the Association of Classical and Christian Schools (ACCS) schools. Among these contenders for the term, the one thing necessary is care in definition. These various schools of thought should not fight for the glory of sole possession, but rather argue in such a way that what everyone means is clear. Put another way, every form of classicism should be able to agree on the importance of early definition of terms in any discussion or debate.

But, unfortunately, because the world is the messy kind of place it is and because America is the kind of place *it* is, we should also expect to find various knock-offs and counterfeits. One common practice is simply to take whatever the school was already doing and simply call it *classical*. Another less-than-adequate approach introduces just enough of a classical touch (one elective, say, on Latin word origins) to persuade inquiring parents that a classical education is being provided. In the long run, it is not necessary to engage such practices in debate, for, as Cicero would have said (had he thought of it), the proof is in the pudding.

In their survey of the classical school resurgence, Gene Veith and Andrew Kern provide the valuable service of identifying differences and similarities in the various legitimate classical approaches. For example, they compare the classical Christian approach with the democratic classicism advocated by Adler.

> There are significant differences between the ACCS and the Paideia schools. ACCS questions the validity of state schooling; by contrast, the Paideia proposal is specifically geared to the reform of public schools. Religion is foundational to the ACCS curriculum, and Christianity is the point of integration through which all knowledge is made complete. Paideia does not dismiss the importance of religion, but its approach is more secular, and its foundational value is democracy. If the approach of ACCS can be described as Christian classicism, Paideia's can best be described as democratic classicism.[1]

Various aspects of this proposal have already been discussed in earlier chapters. Here it is only important to point out that the *Paideia* proposal, as a great books program, is a legitimately *classical* approach to education. But for classical Christian educators, "classical" is not enough. We want our schools to be thoroughly and rigorously Christian as well.

Then there is elite classicism. For one example, Thomas Jefferson School in St. Louis offers a rigorous elite education. But is it classical? On one of their brochures they answer the question this way:

> The term "classical" implies different things to different people. The subjects we teach and the works we include in our syllabi are, for the most part, time-tested and acknowledged as important by most educated people and by American colleges. But the material, or the approach to it, may in some cases be as new as the current year. An English class may study Maya Angelou alongside Shakespeare. In biology class, the student will not only gain a knowledge of anatomy, accumulated over centuries, but will also learn about the latest advances in knowledge of the human genome. A student reading the *Odyssey* in Greek will not only be sharing an experience that goes back 2,500 years but will also be viewing Odysseus and his adventures through the eyes of a 21st-century citizen. We leave it to each reader to decide whether our program fits his or her own definition of a classical education.[2]

Not only is the education rigorous, but the classical and time-tested aspects of the curriculum are mixed in an eclectic way with more modern elements—Maya Angelou alongside Shakespeare. Of course, some might say this is not a mixture of modern and ancient, but rather a mixture of the time-tested and the trendy. Still, the parents of students enrolled in such academies are paying, ahem, significant amounts in tuition, and they are not doing this in order to get illiterate kids back. The standards are clearly very high. But at the same time, the standards are high because of the social position of the families of the students and the social position of the school. In the other classical academies the standards are high because the schools are trying to recapture something, take something back. With some of the more well-heeled, established schools the standards are high because the schools inherited such standards.

Veith and Kern point to another classical approach, which might be called moral classicism. The leader in this movement is David Hicks. In his book *Norms and Nobility* he sets out his approach to education. Veith and Kern discuss Adler's *Paideia* proposal, the ACCS approach, and the Hicks approach. Or if we think of them in terms of their pedagogical ancestry, the Aristotelian approach, the Augustinian approach, and the Platonic approach.

> If the ACCS offers a Christian classicism and Paideia champions a democratic classicism, Hicks can be described as a spokesman for a moral classicism. Each approach to classicism described here rests on somewhat different philosophical foundations, though their intentions and methods are quite similar and compatible. Douglas Wilson is an Augustinian: his school teaches that which can be known with systematic rigor, but it does so with an awareness of human sin, the need for God's grace and sovereignty over all of life, positions that characterize Wilson's specifically Reformed, Calvinist theology. . . . Mortimer Adler is an Aristotelian, and the Paideia proposal reflects the scrutiny of purpose, making of distinctions, and commonsense rationalism that are Aristotle's legacy to Western thought. Hicks finds his inspiration in Plato. He builds his educational theory around a search for the ideal and a conviction that education should be a path to virtue. His curriculum is akin to the classical humanism of the Renaissance, which studies the humanistic disciplines to cultivate man's potential.[3]

The ACCS approach to education is specifically and distinctively Christian, and hence it is more dogmatic and settled than what either Adler or Hicks would propose. The purpose of an open mind, the Christian classicists would say, paraphrasing Chesterton, is the same as the purpose of an open mouth—it is meant to *close* on something. While ACCS schools vary among themselves in their doctrinal commitments—some are Reformed, some more Lutheran, and others are confessional evangelical—they all would glory in their doctrinal commitment, seeing that commitment as the only way to gain educational traction in a slippery world.

Hick's and Adler's approaches have in common a dedication to dialectic in education. "The first characteristic of a classical school, according to Hicks, is its reliance on dialectic."[4]

For ACCS schools, dialectic is one part of the educational process but not a first principle. The goal in classical Christian schools is to move from grammar to dialectic, and then from dialectic on to rhetoric. To remain in the dialectic would be considered a failure.

The goals vary as well. Adler would want to train students to be able to participate in the great conversation with intelligence and grace. While not differing with this, Hicks would want more of an emphasis on moral improvement. "Hick's goal is to restore to education norms—standards of morality and excellence—and to education, the elevation of young students to lives of virtue and achievement."[5]

So, then, what is the definition of classical education? It is important to understand that I am giving a stipulated definition. In no way do I begrudge other legitimate uses of the phrase. In other words, classical education, as *I* am using the phrase, refers to a particular pedagogical approach together with an emphasis on passing on the heritage of the West. The pedagogy refers to our commitment to Dorothy Sayers's basic insight—that children grow naturally through stages that correspond nicely with the three elements of the Trivium. We teach the grammar of all subjects to the younger children; we teach dialectic to the children of junior-high age; and we teach the rhetorical disciplines to the high school students.

At the same time, Western culture receives the emphasis it does because this is the culture in which the Christian faith has made the greatest advances. Western civilization is not synonymous with the kingdom of God, but the histories of the two entities are so intertwined that one cannot be understood apart from the other. Try to imagine a decent history of the West that made no reference to Christianity or a church history that made no mention of Charlemagne or Constantine. We do not teach Western culture in a jingoistic fashion; rather, we believe that students who are taught to love their own culture will understand why other people love theirs. A man who honors his mother understands another man honoring *his*. In contrast, our society's multicultural experiment attempts to teach children to respect the cultures of others by instilling in them a practical contempt for their own. But global harmony will take far more than occasional food fairs with samples of international spicy foods.

While classical Christian schools need not be confessionally Reformed in their doctrinal commitments, it is essential that all classical Christian schools not be hostile to this historic Protestant approach. The reasons for this should become apparent in the coming chapters.

10

LOGOS SCHOOL, ACCS, AND NEW ST. ANDREWS

TWENTY YEARS AFTER its founding, Logos School continues to flourish. Moscow, Idaho, is not a large town, and the fact that a private school the size of Logos (around three hundred students now) can operate successfully here is a testimony to the quality of the work that is being done.

We founded Logos in the early eighties because we wanted our children to receive a better education than we had received. God has blessed these efforts, and my wife and I are now contemplating the prospect of our grandchildren beginning their course of study there in just a few years.

When the school was founded, we adopted the motto, "A Classical and Christ-centered Education." We were not sure of all the ramifications, but we took on the motto because we did not want the school to be a reactionary fundamentalist academy (hence, *classical*). At the same time we did not want the school to be disconnected from the historic Christian faith (hence, *Christ-centered*).

In the course of our early research on what our founding pedagogical vision would be, I remembered having read Dorothy Sayers's essay entitled "The Lost Tools of Learning," which had been reprinted in *National Review*. A faithful subscriber, I had read it first during my time in the navy—although I was a bachelor at the time, without any thoughts of Christian education to trouble me. I hunted down the article again later, and it seemed to be just what we needed. Dorothy Sayers said in the essay that she did not believe there was anyone crazy enough to actually try what she was suggesting, but we were not so easily put off.

A worldview is like a cheap sweater (or a good sweater too, for that matter). If you pull on a loose strand found on your left arm, it is not long before your right arm begins to unravel. Everything is connected. Pedagogy is connected to theology, which is connected to worship, which is connected to politics, and so on. In the complacent era of American evangelicalism that had followed the Second World War, it was possible for Christians to gather together for one morning a week, with one of their number selected to speak for a small portion of that time. This was a workable proposition, and we all thought that we had the whole counsel of God.

But in the seventies and eighties, Christian parents began taking the task of education seriously. And what happens when you establish a school? One of the first things you discover is that the kids show up five days a week, eight hours a day, for nine months out of the year, for twelve years. *You have to have something to say.* A weekly homily won't cut it.

This means either one of two things. The first option is just to copy what the world is saying down the street at their free school. But dissatisfaction with that course of study is what brought about the establishment of this school in the first place. And, moreover, if we are going to say all the same things, why pay the extra tuition to do it?

The other option is to give yourself to the acquisition of a thoroughgoing biblical life- and worldview. And this is what happened at Logos. The more we studied and learned, the more we realized how far we had to go. And the process is still continuing—from the raising of cultural standards within the school to refinements in the application of the Trivium. God has greatly blessed the school, far beyond our deserving, and we are grateful to Him for it.

Even more encouraging than the fact that Logos has stayed faithful to the vision established at the beginning is the fact that the administrators and teachers there have taken the lead in defining and refining that classical vision. Far from experiencing mission drift, the administration at Logos is more dedicated than ever to the work of repairing the ruins. When the school was first founded, the outside world knew nothing about us. A handful of teachers and a slightly larger handful of students in a church basement did not make everyone stop and stare. A few years later, when the school acquired a building of its own, it occupied the place of "generic" private school in the minds of many. For some, it was just that "Jesus freak" school. But now with a growing national reputation, the school is known for academic excellence locally as well. This good reputation is remarkable in that it was not achieved through any kind of compromise. Quite the reverse.

After we had been at the work for about a decade, the opportunity came for me to write *Recovering the Lost Tools of Learning*, which was part of the Turning Point worldview series published by Crossway Books and the Fieldstead Institute. That series of books sought to apply a biblical worldview to all manner of subjects—film, popular music, foreign policy, journalism, environmentalism, and so on. Marvin Olasky was the editor of the series and was kind enough to recommend to his board that I write their book on education.

We did not really anticipate what would follow. When someone read the book on film, they would then go to the movies with a more biblical perspective. If someone read the book on foreign policy, they would seek to vote more intelligently. But when they read *Recovering*, they said, "Hey, let's start a school!" Soon I began to get requests in the mail. The volume of mail grew to the point that my wife, Nancy, had to take over my education correspondence. Eventually we decided that we needed to found an organization to handle all the requests.

It would be nice to say that this decision was the result of a broad visionary insight, but we made it out of pure self-defense as much as anything. We needed to create an institution that could process the inquiries and help those parents who were crazy enough to start a classical school. Hence the birth of ACCS. The initial board included Marlin Detweiler, Tom Spencer, and, as the Victorians used to say, the present writer.

The ACCS sponsors an annual national conference in the summer, with plenary talks designed to challenge and motivate and workshops designed to instruct in various applications of the classical and Christian approach. The ACCS also has begun the necessary work of accrediting classical and Christian schools. The curriculum and vision of our schools is so distinct that existing accreditation bodies could not really evaluate what we are trying to do. The organization publishes a regular newsletter entitled *Classis*. Over one hundred schools around the nation (and a few overseas) make up the ACCS.

Those interested in starting a school or in turning a school in a classical direction should not do anything without knowing what resources are available from ACCS. For just one example, we have a notebook available for those "starting up." The association is under the very capable leadership of executive director Patch Blakey and under the authority of a national board representing classical Christian schools around the country.[1] In short, the Association of Classical and Christian Schools is an invaluable resource for those thinking about starting a classical Christian school, those in the middle of it already, and those associated with a more traditional school that is considering the classical model.

Another great need is for information about where to get classical materials, teacher training material, and textbooks. One of the things that ACCS does is refer schools to these providers. Three important resources offer most of what a beginning school needs. First, Logos School publishes many of the materials that they have generated in their classrooms. A descriptive catalog of curriculum guides and materials is available.[2] A second great resource for texts and background pedagogical materials on the theory of classical and Christian education is Canon Press.[3] A third resource, the "big mama" of classical and Christian materials, is Veritas Press. They are a full-service curriculum provider for both classical Christian schools and homeschools.[4] If they don't have it, you were probably in sin for wanting it in the first place.

But there was one other unexpected consequence of all these developments, and it was the formation of New St. Andrews College. One thing leads to another, as they say, and we eventually discovered that our graduates of Logos were all dressed up with no place to go. My longsuffering daughter Bekah, who entered Logos School in kindergarten the year it opened, also entered New St. Andrews College as a freshman the year *it* opened as a four-year school.

Some might wonder at the comment that there "was no place to go." The American landscape is covered with Christian colleges, but these colleges (overwhelmingly) have two major problems. When Bekah was still in high school, she began to receive mailings from Christian colleges. From the brochures, it would be fair to conclude that the purpose of attending an evangelical Christian college is to ride horses, eat pizza, and make lifetime friends. In other words, it was hardly a clarion call to academic discipline, integrity, and hard work. At least one college I know of has a Dean of Fun.

The other problem is rooted more deeply and is harder to address. The profound sense of the antithesis that Christian parents develop over the course of educating their sons and daughters is largely missing from the evangelical establishment in higher education. From compromise on evolution, to compromise on egalitarianism, to compromise on secular accrediting standards, today's Christian colleges in America are an epistemological mess. Christian colleges are a major part of our problem.[5]

And so we began offering classes toward a B.A. in liberal arts and culture. One degree, one course of study, one diploma. As Henry Ford said, you can have the car in any color so long as it is black. The first year NSA had four students, including our daughter. At the time of writing this, we have over one hundred students from around thirty states and a few Canadian provinces.

The college has been able to attract high-caliber instructors and is under the effective leadership of Dean Roy Atwood. The significance of this college is plain to everyone who has been involved in starting up a classical or Christian school. The single, greatest need in the classical Christian movement is trained teachers. NSA has made great strides toward its goal of graduating around thirty students a year, thoroughly trained in a Christian worldview and the classical languages. Many of the current graduates are already teaching in classical Christian schools around the country—from Delaware to Seattle.

The demand for our teachers is not surprising, given that the students are required to take four years of language study. A year and a half of Latin and another year and a half of Greek are required. The remaining year can be spent in additional study of Latin or Greek, or students may take a year of Hebrew. In addition to their language studies, freshman take a year-long course in classical rhetoric, along with another year of what is called the lordship class—basic worldview thinking in every area of life. The students also study world history, with particular emphasis on ancient history. Yet other year-long courses are biblical theology and music—the latter being frankly weak on the electric bass guitar. Another heavy emphasis is literature.

God has been very kind to us, not only in the day of small beginnings, but in the day of three small beginnings. With Logos, with ACCS and all the schools represented there, and with New St. Andrews College, we have been blessed beyond all reckoning.

ANTITHESIS

11

THE CHRISTIAN HEART AND MIND

MARK TWAIN ONCE HAD an exchange with his long-suffering wife, who had finally had enough of his swearing and cursing. So one day she walked up to him and calmly repeated back to him every such word she had ever heard him use. When she was done, he looked at her and said, "My dear, you know the words, but you don't know the tune." In like manner, many Christians have gotten into the business of worldview education, and judging from the publications, books, conferences, organizations, and general verbal activity, we *have* learned a lot of the words—*worldview, paradigm, epistemology, Trivium,* and so on. But in some key respects we still have not learned the tune.

What is a Christian worldview? To answer the question, we have to begin with what it is not. And in some of the subtle cases, we have to consider what a Christian worldview *almost* is. In the first place, a Christian worldview is not the same thing as Christian worldview jargon. The oldest trick in the world is to attach oneself to some promising movement or other by simply putting on the uniform and leaving the gun at home. Talking imitatively, without understanding, is not all that difficult.

Secondly, and this is crucial, a Christian worldview is not a condiment added to a plate full of neutral food in order to flavor it. The faith of our fathers is not an educational afterthought. The "potatoes" always come from *somebody's* kitchen. Sometimes Hindus, Muslims, and atheists can be induced to eat Christian potatoes (because the Christian education provided at the school is outstanding), but far more common is the practice of Christians eating unbelieving agnostic potatoes with lots of gravy slathered on to cover the smell.

Third, a Christian worldview does not somehow automatically "sanitize" the world so that we can all go watch any R-rated movie we want now, for any reason we want, because "we have a Christian worldview." Put bluntly, a Christian worldview is not an excuse for compromised sinning. A Christian worldview is not an all-purpose disinfectant.

Positively, having a Christian worldview means living as an obedient Christian in all of life—heart, mind, fingers, and toes. A worldview is not a set of rationalistic spectacles we put on that enables us to see the world rightly despite the fuzzy vision caused by disobedience. Our worldview is related to our eyes, obviously, but these eyes are intimately connected with hands, heart, and mind. The Scriptures speak of God as the One who tries the "heart and reins" of men. Our metaphor for this would be God testing the "head and heart," the reason and emotions. But in the ancient Hebrew metaphor, the heart was the seat of the intellect, and the reins— the kidneys—were the seat of the affections. So while Scripture does distinguish reason and emotion, it does not separate them the way we tend to do. They are both located in what C. S. Lewis, in his great book on education entitled *The Abolition of Man*, called "the chest." Our thoughts do not float on the surface of our lives, like leaves that fall on a pond.

When we are walking in obedience to the Gospel, worshiping and living as God requires us to do—hearing His Word, singing His psalms, eating at His table, honoring our parents, loving our wives, respecting our husbands, teaching our children because we cherish them, mowing the lawn when we should, and *also* reading and teaching our history, science, literature, and so on—then we have a Christian worldview. At that point, and not before, our children are safe under our instruction. At that point, the schools we build will be fit for the presence of covenant children.

Considered from another angle, education should not be understood as merely a cerebral affair. This pitfall cannot be avoided merely by adding physical education (although that is important). The well-trained mind is certainly involved in classical Christian education—necessarily so. But certain questions should always arise in our hearts—the mind is trained along with what else, trained in accordance with what, by what standard? Unless faithful worship of the living God is at the center of our lives and our communities, and therefore at the center of our children's education, "Christian worldview education" will simply be one more hollow, intellectualistic experiment. The living God knows that our troubled and flailing generation does not need any more of those. We do not need any more born-again Christian souls thinking pagan thoughts, locked away inside pagan bodies, jobs, hands, clothes, cars, and houses. The Word of God is not chained. The Gospel transforms everything it touches, and the fact that so little in our modern evangelical circles is transformed means simply that the Gospel hasn't touched those circles yet.

Our approach to classical Christian education should be motivated by obedience to Paul's requirement to establish in our midst the *paideia* of the Lord (Eph. 6:4). The end result of this kind of education, properly conceived and implemented, is nothing less than Christian civilization. Christian worship leads to Christian dining rooms, Christian schools, Christian communities, Christian nations. Incidentally, in the Great Commission, this is what Jesus said to do—disciple the nations. When proponents of a Christian worldview settle for anything less, it is not fully a Christian worldview, and in some cases it is not a Christian worldview at all. With this contextual introduction, I draw on a definition of a Christian worldview from my book *The Paideia of God*: "*the framework of assumptions about reality, all of which are in submission to Christ.*"[1] In *Repairing the Ruins* I elaborate further:

> The truth is that there is no secular/sacred distinction. "The earth is the Lord's, and the fulness thereof" (1 Cor. 10:26). Consequently, we cannot protect and preserve any truth by isolating it from the rest of God's world. To do so kills it. The division is not between the secular and the sacred, between theology and literature. The antithesis is between seeing the entire world the way God says to see it, or refusing to see the entire world the way God says to see it.[2]

The Christian heart and mind are dedicated to the antithesis that God (by definition) has placed in the world He made. The concept of antithesis should be a central organizing feature of every Christian curriculum.

How does this work? God is by definition a given. God could not "not be." He is what philosophers would call a necessary being, in no way a contingent being. Their language is not our language of choice, but we should still get the point. God does not depend upon us for His existence. We, and everything else, depend upon Him. But once God decided to create a contingent universe, we find ourselves with what we call the Creator/creature divide. This is a fundamental ontological division. God is not a larger version of us, only bigger and smarter. The Christian faith does not point to God as a Homeric deity like Zeus—an overgrown celebrity.

Once the triune God created a world that would come to contain evil, He established what we call the *antithesis*. The biblical language describing this divide is found in Genesis 3:15: "And I will put enmity between thee and the woman, and between thy seed and her seed; it shall bruise thy head, and thou shalt bruise his heel." The language is not limited to one passage or one period in history but is pervasive throughout Scripture. Jesus calls His enemies a brood of vipers (Matt. 23:33); Paul says the God of peace will soon crush Satan beneath the Romans' feet (Rom. 16:20); the Bible ends with a climactic battle with that "ancient serpent" (Rev. 20:2). The entire Bible is about this curse, and we are told in Scripture that the rest of post-biblical history is dominated by the same curse. We see then that the antithesis is not a study in morally neutral contrasts, and so it teaches us to expect antipathy.

So the antithesis is a given. But because it is, some will always try to misplace the antithesis. In other words, they affirm it in principle but misapply it in practice. Misplacing it is really the first of two basic ways to try to get away from this antithesis between the seed of the serpent and the seed of the woman, between faith and unbelief, between covenant-keepers and covenant-breakers. People misplace the antithesis by affirming the fundamental divide between good and evil but then misdrawing the lines of that divide. The lines are thought to be tribal or racial or political. Misplacing the antithesis is the besetting sin of secular conservatives.

But the liberal method is to deny that there is an antithesis. "We are all saying the same *thing* really! C'mon, people, now smile on your brother, etc." This tendency is very popular in these days, and it explains the common treatment of Christians. If there is no antithesis in the world, then the one intolerable thing is to insist that there is. The default divide therefore comes between one group that says there is no antithesis and the "wicked others" who maintain that there is. Two groups: One says that it is true that there is no truth, and the other group says that that's not true.

Another (common) conservative sin in this regard is that of thinking that the antithesis can be expressed in a wooden, simplistic, jargon-ridden approach to right and wrong—the paradise of legalists. But a belief that truth is absolute is not the same thing as saying that truth is simple. Because God knows all things exhaustively, He knows (for any given situation) the right thing to do. He knows which course of action is *ultimately* wise. I need not know everything, but the fact that God knows everything enables me to know *something*. In the same way, the fact that God knows the fault lines of antithesis in everything enables me to make progress.

Now we come to the curriculum. When we set ourselves to teach the biblical worldview in the classroom, we will often be taunted by those who know that we do not know everything. We sometimes let the shaft go home because we know that is true. It is worse than this: We *actually* do not even know everything about the dung beetle. If we do not know everything about a lowly bug, then how can we claim to be operating on the basis of a knowledge of ultimate good and evil—on the basis of the antithesis? But the problem with this question is that a Christian worldview is confused with a "God's-eye view."

Here we see the importance of Scripture. We don't have to figure out the fundamentals for ourselves. God has given us His Word, and it was *tailored* for our circumstances. This is why remembering the antithesis is so important in our understanding of the doctrines of Scripture. First, Satan questioned the reliability and veracity of God's Word: "Yea, hath God said?" (Gen. 3:1). The liberal does this. He blurs the antithesis between the binding Word of God and the nonbinding words of men. But the other escape route is the conservative one (again): God's Word is affirmed in theory but ignored in practice.

Every Christian school must adopt an implicit, absolute, childlike wonder at the glory of the Scriptures. We must be people of the Book, knowing it top to bottom, front to back. And we must resolve, before the fact, to have absolutely no problem with any passage of Scripture once the meaning of that passage has been ascertained through honest exegesis. This means, among other things, that Christians must be prepared to condemn sodomy, embrace the doctrine of creation, say that husbands are the heads of their wives, believe in giants and dragons, and believe in Noah's ark right down to, if necessary, the giraffe's head sticking out the window.

God's Word is pure. But the idea of the purity of the "ultimate word" is actually inescapable. All creatures must locate the ultimate somewhere.

Why not in God's Word? The alternative is man's word. This "take no prisoners" approach is really the only one open to us.

> Our Savior has also declared that there is no moral neutrality—he that is not with Him is against Him. Combined with this, consider that every man is born in a state of alienation from God. Practical enmity and atheism are the natural outgrowth of this disposition. The only remedy for this natural disease of a man's spirit is gospel truth. The comparison of these truths will make it perfectly plain that a non-Christian training must be literally an anti-Christian training.[3]

Such a view can come across as biblicist fire-breathing, but really it is just a matter of stone-cold reason. The claims of the Christian faith are total. If those total claims are erroneous, then the faith is false. We can illustrate by pointing to what it sounds like when we state the opposite out loud. Not surprisingly, Adler provides a good example. He said, "Only the liberal arts can provide the standard for judging excellence in teaching, for measuring the efficiency of educational means, or for inventing others; and *the liberal arts are neither pagan nor Christian, but human*."[4] This statement amounts to saying that we should let Cicero talk, and Socrates, and Augustine, and so on. We should hear them all out. But we cannot at the end of the day, on the basis of our discussion, make a decision about how to live.

The Christian heart and mind, in short, finds this approach incoherent.

> Every line of true knowledge must find its completeness as it converges on God, just as every beam of daylight leads the eye to the sun. If religion is excluded from our study, every process of thought will be arrested before it reaches its proper goal. The structure of thought must remain a truncated cone, with its proper apex lacking.[5]

12

THE PEERS PROBLEM

IT WOULD BE NICE indeed if worldview problems could be solved by just crossing the street and opening up a new school, one that is all fresh and clean. But the difficulty is that we track stuff in with us. Wherever we go, there we are.

The antithesis that exists between light and darkness extends to every area of life. Since we are not withdrawing to the wilderness to establish Hermitage Christian School, we must continue to deal with the world around us as we seek to establish biblical education. And because the world around us resembles a particularly persistent and thick fog, some of it gets *in*. Some of the ways this infiltration takes place will be discussed further in subsequent chapters, but the subject of this chapter is the fact of infiltration. Despite the best efforts of parents, educators, and administrators, worldliness seeps into our schools. In a significant number of cases, worldly thinking *floods* into our schools.

One organization, the Nehemiah Institute, is dedicated to monitoring this problem, and they have developed the PEERS test as their main instrument for this purpose. PEERS testing "categorizes beliefs in Politics, Economics, Education, Religion, and Social Issues (PEERS) into one of four worldview classifications: Biblical Theism, Moderate Christian, Secular Humanism, or Socialism."[1]

Our discussion of this test should begin with at least two significant caveats. The first is that even though modernity likes to categorize all data through quantification, not everything fits neatly into such categories. Christians should always beware of overconfident quantified assertions. For example, some readers might be wondering if a worldview can have a number assigned to it. Isn't this a bit like saying a student has ten pounds of poetic ability or five yards of charm? The answer is to acknowledge that this is a very real problem, and we have to guard against being overly precise in areas that do not permit such an approach. Yet, as children of modernity, we are accustomed to this process in everything else we do, and wise men and women know how to supply the necessary discount. (Some of the other more detailed issues with regard to this quantification in grading and evaluation will be discussed in a later chapter.)

The second qualification has to do with anticipated disagreements about the answer to this or that question. In other words, suppose the folks grading the test mark an answer "wrong." They are in effect saying that the answer was wrong *and* unbiblical. This is fine, the objector might be saying, if we are talking about the deity of Christ. But suppose the question was on economics? "Are these people saying I am less of a Christian if I disagree with their particular objections to wage and price controls?" This criticism also has a legitimate point. Sometimes the questions on the PEERS test reflect more of a conservative political flavor than a thoroughly biblical worldview.

But even with such criticisms acknowledged, the test can still be used with great profit by administrators and teachers who use it wisely. Suppose an entire teaching staff of committed Christians takes the test, and their average score is 85. This means that on average these good Christians disagree with the good Christians at the Nehemiah Institute 15 percent of the time. But this is no reason for everyone to throw down their number 2 pencils and walk off in disgust. The test is still *very* informative. Let us say that the *students* in that same school averaged at about 45. This tells us (if it tells us nothing else) that the worldview of the teachers is not getting passed on to the students very well. The disparity between the views the teachers and the views of the students means that someone is not communicating.

With all this said, the questions on the whole *do* represent basic Christian convictions. Here are some sample questions taken at random from the test. The questions are simple indicative statements, and the students have to register the extent of their agreement or disagreement.

• "Human life as a real and unique person begins at conception" (p. 5).

• "Premarital sex is always wrong and should not be condoned by society" (p. 6).

- "Centralized government is inefficient and is counterproductive for society as a whole" (p. 4).
- "The major obstacles to social progress are ignorance and faulty social institutions" (p. 4).
- "The most effective way of curbing inflation is for the government to impose wage and price controls" (p. 5).[2]

Confronted with statements like this, the student has five options for each question. First, he can "strongly agree," which means "this is the truth. [He has] a conviction that the statement is correct in all ways; [he] would defend it without compromise."

Or he might want to qualify his response and "tend to agree." This means basically "[he agrees] with the statement. [He] may not completely understand the subject, and [he] may not want to debate it, but it seems more right than wrong."

Or he might want to say the equivalent of *max nix*. He is "neutral." "[He does] not understand the statement; [he has] no opinion about the issue; [he thinks] the issue is irrelevant to daily life."

Moving into the opposition column, he might "tend to disagree." "The statement does not sound right to [him] but [he is] not sure [he] could prove it wrong."

Or we might put him in the ranks of the strongly opposed. This answer is "strongly disagree." "[He is] firmly convinced the statement is false. [He has] a conviction, not just a preference, that the statement is in total error and that [he] could defend the opposite viewpoint."[3]

Now given the nature of such questions and this range of possible answers, it would be difficult to miss a student's basic worldview orientation. If any are still unsure, perhaps if we stopped thinking of it as a test and simply considered it more as a thorough, probing *interview*, we would be able to see how valuable such information actually is. Think again of the questions: If the majority of students in a Christian academy "tended to disagree" with the sentiment that sex before marriage was wrong, then it is clear that these students are getting their convictions about right and wrong from a source other than the Bible. If they are from Christian homes, and they attend a Christian school, where are they getting it?

To their credit, the Nehemiah Institute handles the data they get from these tests carefully, which is to say that they are not gnat-stranglers.

The poor fellow who disagreed with them about wage and price controls is not written off as a flaming atheist. According to their scale, 70 and above ranks as biblical theism. A score of 30 to 69 is considered moderately Christian. But 0 to 29 is secular humanist. There is no reason to assume that a difference of opinion about this particular question or that one is the watershed between atheism and Christianity.

But now for the bad news. How do the kids from Christian schools do, compared to Christian students in government schools? The testing began in the mid-eighties. And since that time, all the indicators are that Christian students in the government schools have lost the battle, and that students in traditional Christian schools are right behind them. For example, in 1988 the composite score for Christians in the government schools was 36.1. In the year 2001, it was 7.5. Christian students in Christian schools in 1988 scored at 47.2. But in 2001 they were at 22.4. *Both of these categories* saw students go from a moderate Christian perspective to a secular humanist perspective. If that is what is going to happen anyway, then why pay tuition to go to a Christian school? If someone is resolved to drive over a cliff, shouldn't the person want the car to go faster, not slower?

What the Nehemiah Institute calls "worldview schools" are the exception to this unhappy pattern. In 1988 the composite score in such a school was 61.2. In 2001 it was 70.1, now ranking these schools, on average, in the biblical theism category. This is still not as good as it could be, but it is not a rout. These schools are holding their own.[4] Christian students in government schools come to share the worldview of their teachers—not the worldview of their families or their churches. Christian students in the average, generic Christian school fare little better.

> However, with nearly each subsequent year of testing, we found the understanding of the Christian worldview by students to be lower than the year before. This trend has continued through year 2001. The only exceptions to the decline were Christian schools that had adopted specific worldview materials in their curriculum. These are primarily schools known as Principle Approach or Classical Christian, and home-schools. I believe students from these schools represent the true remnant and hope for the future, but they represent less than 5% of total students tested.[5]

G. K. Chesterton once commented that a man must stand for something, or he will fall for anything. We see the truth of that statement here. Educators with a *defined* worldview commitment that serves as a structuring point for their curriculum are successful in passing that worldview on to their students. Classical Christian schools do this. Principle Approach schools do this. Many homeschools do it. But this result does not come about automatically because someone has pulled out of the government school system.

Another possible objection to the PEERS test is that it may not be representative enough. But the Nehemiah Institute has been doing testing for some time, and the information they have collected is of enormous significance. Their testing has involved approximately 15,000 students from all fifty states, and the results show that most Christian schools do *not* successfully inculcate a Christian view of life and culture.

> I will add here that results of PEERS testing over the past decade show that a wide difference in Biblical worldview understanding exists even among Christian schools. For a host of reasons, the humanist worldview has found its way into Christian education. We cannot just move our students to a different school setting, add prayer and a chapel service, and expect the problem of humanism to disappear.[6]

The determining factor is not how conservative the teachers and administrators are. In one special study of *sixty* very conservative schools, the results were dismaying. A total of 67.2 percent of the students tested at secular humanist levels, while 32.8 percent were moderate Christian—at the lower end of moderate Christian. Just a few more years, and they will be joining their friends who have gone over to the adversary.[7] A conservative institution can fail to pass on its values, and this appears to be what is occurring. Chesterton's statement should come back to haunt us. We will fall for anything.

13

THE *PAIDEIA* OF GOD

NOT ALL WORDS ARE created equal. All cultures have certain words in which they invest all their collective cultural capital. In our time, an ordinary word would be something like *shoelace* or *doorknob*. But other words carry a lot more freight for modern people—words such as *democracy*. The fact that some of us are more than a little suspicious of democracy does not alter the fact that our culture is democratic and has entrusted its heart and soul to the concept.

The same thing was true in the ancient world. Certain words were quite pedestrian—they had shoelaces too—while others were an embodiment of all their cultural values. One of the great words for them was *paideia*. "The word *paideia* goes far beyond the scope and sequence of what we call *formal* education. In the ancient world, the *paideia* was all-encompassing and involved nothing less than the enculturation of the future citizens."[1] The *paideia* extends well past the simple limits of an established curriculum; it describes an entire way of life. In short, the ancients understood that education was religious and that religious claims are total.

The ideal education for the sophisticated pagan was one in which the student was prepared to take his place in the city/state and to discharge his obligations there. This process of enculturation was all-encompassing, including every aspect of a student's life. The Roman rhetor Quintilian even went so far as to say that parents should take care to hire a nursemaid who pronounced words properly. Words heard by a toddler were an important part of that child's education. A child learned lessons in school certainly, but he was also being assimilated into the culture of his city when he worshiped the gods at their festivals, walked to school past their temples, and learned to put on a toga a certain way.

Looking ahead to our conclusion, we should note that the apostle Paul required the fathers of Ephesus to provide a peculiarly Christian *paideia* for their children (Eph. 6:4). But before considering the ramifications in greater detail, we have to learn more about what the *paideia* meant in the ancient pagan world. Werner Jaeger points to the comprehensiveness of the word.

> Ever since the age of the sophists, all the leaders of Greek *paideia*, and above all Plato and Isocrates, agreed in deciding that *paideia* should not be limited to school-teaching. To them it was culture, the formation of the human soul. That is what differentiates Greek *paideia* from the educational system of other nations. It was an absolute ideal.[2]

They set their sights high. Aristotle employed the word *psychikos* to describe men and women at their best, the end product of the process of *paideia*. This was a person entirely equipped to assume his or her station of service to the *polis*. The antithesis between this pagan notion and the biblical approach can be seen in the apostle Paul's diatribe against pagan philosophy in the first two chapters of 1 Corinthians. In my view, this entire section should be understood as Paul's critique of Aristotle—and anyone else like him. Paul uses the same word *psychikos* to describe a person who is spiritually clueless. What for Aristotle was the highest compliment he could offer was for Paul the description of a person blind to the things of God. He says, "the natural man receiveth not the things of the Spirit of God: for they are foolishness unto him: neither can he know them, because they are spiritually discerned" (1 Cor. 2:14). Modern Christians think of a "natural man" as a drug addict or libertine. But Paul was not describing the Corinthian skid row; he was attacking the philosophy department at the University of Athens. "Where is the wise? where is the scribe? where is the disputer of this world? hath not God made foolish the wisdom of this world?" (1 Cor. 1:20).

Paul was not opposed to the idea of the *paideia*. He was opposed to a *paideia* built on the foundations of autonomous human wisdom. He did not, as many anti-intellectual Christians have done, reject the life of the mind. What he did was reject the idea that the life of the mind can in any way be sustained apart from salvation in Christ and a sure word from God.

By the first century, the inadequacy of the autonomous *paideia* also had begun to dawn on the pagans themselves. This is one of the reasons that the Christian faith was preached with such success. The autonomous *paideia* was for the ancients an idol that had failed them. Or, to use a different analogy, it was a house built on sand. The idolatrous assumptions of paganism could not support the weight placed upon them. Christopher Dawson comments: "From the time of Plato the Hellenic *paideia* was a humanism in search of a theology, and the religious traditions of Greek culture were neither deep nor wide enough to provide the answer."[3]

Dawson goes on to show the result of the failure of this *paideia:* "The new Christian culture was therefore built from the beginning on a double foundation."[4] But I would argue that the ancient *paideia* was not foundational (in principle) to the developing Christian culture, but rather a teaching in need of a foundation, as Dawson pointed out a page earlier. To the extent that a true foundational blending did occur, the Christians faced a problem of compromise that became increasingly obvious in the subsequent centuries. We should never tire of repeating that religious claims are total, and as the Christian faith conquered the ancient world, the Christians understood the essential principle that Christ is the foundation of all of life and thought. At the same time, these Christians had to deal with those aspects of the education curriculum taken over from the pagans that were undeniably true. At any rate, the changes brought to the *paideia* were comprehensive and convulsive: "The religious needs of the ancient world were satisfied not by philosophy but by the new religion which had emerged so suddenly and unpredictably from beneath the surface of dominant culture. The coming of Christianity involved great cultural changes both socially and intellectually."[5]

Earlier we noted that the apostle Paul commanded Ephesian fathers to provide their children with a *paideia* of the Lord. This is not a command limited to enrollment in a Christian school. What Paul is requiring is nothing less than the establishment of a Christian civilization or culture. *Paideia* means enculturation, and you cannot have Christian enculturation without a Christian culture. Werner Jaeger makes a pertinent comment here and is worth quoting at length. He is discussing the use made of the term *paideia* by Clement of Rome in his letter to the Corinthians. Clement was a friend of the apostle Paul (Phil. 4:3), and the way he employs the term builds on Hebrew usage (which meant simply *admonition* or *chastisement*).

> But in 62.3 Clement uses the phrase "paideia of God" for the sum total of all the Logia of the written tradition, a use corresponding to the Greek sense of the term. It is used in the same sense in 2 Timothy 3:14-16. It is obvious that under the influence of the existence of the much-admired "Greek paideia," which was common knowledge for all men, a new concept of Christian paideia was being evolved, the further development of which we are going to trace through the following centuries. The remarkable thing is that this process starts in a group of Christian writings that consists of the Epistles to the Ephesians (6:4) and to the Hebrews (12:5), II Timothy (3:14-16), and Clement's letter to the Corinthians. Among them the Epistles to the Ephesians and to the Hebrews mark the first steps in this direction, whereas Clement's epistle to the Corinthians shows a large expansion of this idea and of its application in Christian life and thought. . . . History does not proceed by starting with a definition of what it takes over from the past, but by taking possession of it and adapting it to its new purposes.[6]

The passages cited from the New Testament by Jaeger are as follows:

> *And, ye fathers, provoke not your children to wrath: but bring them up in the nurture and admonition of the Lord. (Eph. 6:4)*

> *And ye have forgotten the exhortation which speaketh unto you as unto children, My son, despise not thou the chastening of the Lord, nor faint when thou art rebuked of him. (Heb. 12:5)*

> *But continue thou in the things which thou hast learned and hast been assured of, knowing of whom thou has learned them; and that from a child thou hast known the holy scriptures, which are able to make thee wise unto salvation through faith which is in Christ Jesus. All scripture is given by inspiration of God, and is profitable for doctrine, for reproof, for correction, for instruction in righteousness. (2 Tim. 3:14-16)*

In Ephesians Paul commands fathers to provide their children with the "paideia of the Lord." In Hebrews the children of God are told not to despise the difficulties of being trained by the Lord in His *paideia*. This course of instruction certainly includes the notion of admonition or chastisement, but according to 2 Timothy, all of Scripture is to be employed in this training process because it is profitable for establishing a *paideia* in righteousness (v. 16). These verses show why classical Christian academies teach all subjects as an integrated whole with the Scriptures at the center. Paul says the Scriptures are profitable as the foundation of our Christian *paideia*. So all these requirements were nothing short of a requirement for a Christian *paideia*, one that brought up Christian girls and boys to maturity in the faith, a maturity that presupposes the need for a Christian culture.

Consequently, many Christians involved in modern Christian education need to adopt a more *comprehensive* vision for education. A Christian education is not a process that dabbles around the edges or tries to improve something in need of radical reformation through a simple rearrangement. We may have seen a student who has a basic problem—he needs to study more. He knows he has a problem, and he resolves to do better. He then spends quite a bit of time and energy on reorganizing his notebook—better grades through putting in notebook dividers! This task, as his mother might point out, is easier than studying.

The above problem lends itself to too many metaphors. Rearranging the furniture is not the same as deep-cleaning the carpet. Too many suggested reforms of education in America are precisely this—a rearranging of the existing furniture. But much more than minor reform is necessary—minor reform is healing the wound lightly. Improving grades through notebook reorganization. Picking up instead of cleaning. We can speak of it in so many ways because it is such a common phenomenon. But true educational reform is nothing less than an insistence on the *paideia* of God. When this *paideia* starts to be established, what will be its general characteristics?

First, education reform cannot be sustained apart from a deep and passionate commitment to the historic Christian faith, lived out in faithful worshiping communities, as was discussed earlier. The Christian school is not at the center of the Christian world—that space is taken by the worship of God on the Lord's Day.

Secondly, education reform cannot occur apart from a love of particular things—children, towns, books, subjects, music, and on and on, to the end of one's life and into the next. Why? God has given us salvation through Christ, who took on His incarnate form during the reign of Caesar Augustus. He grew up in a particular town and suffered under

Pontius Pilate. This particularity is central to a right understanding of the Christian faith. The transcendent God is not irrelevant to this particular classroom. Individuals matter, particular subjects matter.

Third, education reform is not possible apart from faith. This is the spiritual way of putting it, but in the vernacular, education reform cannot happen without a sufficient number of crazy people—those who serve a God who calls things that are not as though they are. God commands Christian education, and He promises to bless our obedience in this area.

Given these principles, what are the possible obstacles to true reform? These things mentioned above could hardly generate any opposition at all—until we seek to implement them. It all sounds wonderful on paper, but when we come to particular application, the story can change quite rapidly. So what will the basis of the opposition be? Among other things, we might note a love of ignorance. Ignorance has many problems attendant to it, but one of its advantages is that ignorance is *comfortable*. Another obstacle is loyalty to a set of contemporary beliefs that conflict with this historic Christian vision. One common example would be the current dependence of many modern evangelicals on the categories and teachings of contemporary psychology. Another obstacle could be the conservative suspicion of anything "new." This suspicion can be admirable, but the mistake here is in thinking that the classical approach is new. It is anything but new.

Some other obstacles are more pedestrian. Starting a school takes money. We might like the idea of opening a school but are too cowardly to face the opposition and controversy we know it will generate—perhaps in our families or churches. One of the reasons for controversy is that classical Christian education cannot happen without discipline (see Heb. 12:5 again!), and discipline in our day is controversial. Controversy seems especially certain when we know that the first recipients of any such discipline would be the pastor's son or the most influential board member's daughter. But again the problem is cowardice.

Simple laziness is another problem, observable in many men who stand aside to watch their wives try to shoulder the responsibility for establishing a suitable education for their children. After a time, the wives burn out because they were not built to shoulder that load. Men were built for it, but unfortunately the men are lazy.

Our coming generation is looking to us expectantly. Are we prepared to love them enough to teach them as though the Christian heart and mind matters in the classroom? God tells us that our covenant children are to be established in the *paideia* of God. Unlike the Ephesian fathers to whom this command was first given, we have a heritage, two thousand years old, in which much of the spade work has already been done. We have something to recover; we have an advantage over them. There is much to learn and a lot that can be recovered. Dawson comments: "I believe the study of Christian culture is the missing link which is essential to supply if the tradition of Western education and Western culture is to survive, for it is only through this study that we can understand how Western culture came to exist and what are the essential values for which it stands."[7]

In seeking to provide our children with a Christian *paideia*, we are not starting from scratch. But if we ignore our heritage, we might as well be.

THE CLASSICAL
CHRISTIAN ANSWER

14

THE SEVEN LIBERAL ARTS

THE SCOPE OF this chapter is extensive, and so perhaps a summary of its direction will be necessary at the very beginning. I am attempting here within a small compass a history of classical Christian education, and we will have to fly at treetop level. Also I draw on many sources—important to demonstrate that classical Christian education for confessing believers is far from a newfangled notion; the Christian commitment to this kind of education has not been intermittent but rather sustained over millennia.

Inspired by the words of the apostle Paul, the early Christians began to think and operate in terms of the *paideia* of God. Clement of Rome was notable in this respect. Some elements of the ancient *paideia* were gathered together by these Christians and arranged in a manner suitable to them. Two of the most influential church fathers who sorted through these issues were Augustine and Cassiodorus. The latter was responsible for organizing elements of the *paideia* into what are now called the seven liberal arts, which he equated with the seven pillars in the house of wisdom (Prov. 9:1).

Some important educational reforms were established in the late medieval period, most notably those undertaken by the Brethren of the Common Life. The pattern of classical education they developed remained through the Reformation, although the early Protestants gave new energy to the concept of the antithesis between unbelieving and believing thought. At the same time, historic confessional Protestants played an important role in continuing and extending the classical tradition of education.

The history of classical education is messy. Because many Greek elements were taken up into the process of education (including the language), it has been too easy for many to assume that the civilizing impetus for our culture has been entirely from the pagan world. For example, Cardinal Newman even goes so far as to credit Homer with being the first great apostle of civilization:

> In the country which has been the fountainhead of intellectual gifts, in the age which preceded or introduced the first formations of human society, in an era scarcely historical, we may dimly discern an almost mythical personage, who, putting out of consideration the actors in Old Testament history, may be called the first Apostle of Civilization. . . . "Seven famous towns contend for Homer dead, Through which the living Homer begged his bread."[1]

But Newman's assessment is too facile, although I differ with such a great man with some trepidation. Many great minds have seen Greek civilization as the ancestor of our own. Dawson appears to agree with Newman when he says that the "classical tradition is, in fact, nothing else than Hellenism."[2] But we have to remember the apostle Paul's analogy of the olive tree. Jewish branches were cut out of the olive tree because of their unbelief, and Gentile branches were grafted in. This engrafting of Greeks altered the taste of the olives, but the root remained—an ancient covenant with Abraham, the root being the Lord Jesus Himself. If we have been following Paul's suggestions, we must not think that the engrafting of Greek branches into the tree makes the root Greek. As he might say, may it never be.

The Hebraic background of Christian education is therefore very important. Isaiah refers to some of the pedagogical methods of his day—line on line, precept on precept—when he challenges those who opposed his prophetic ministry (Isa. 28). Prior to the exile, education among the Jews tended to the informality natural to an agrarian society. There were schools for prophets, but general education was connected to the home and involved all of life, crafts, and music.[3] While the Jews were in exile, they saw the operation of Babylonian schools and recognized how these could be adapted to peculiar Jewish concerns. "During their captivity the Jews had an opportunity to see schools for higher training, which were well developed in Babylon."[4] The synagogue began to develop in the exile, in part as a means of maintaining cultural identity in a strange land. It is important to note that the synagogue school grew to be an essential part of the synagogue.

An elementary school developed within the synagogue where children were taught to read and write and to understand simple parts of the law. This institution began sometime in the third century B.C. as an answer to the needs of the people. It grew in importance as its functions were increased. . . . After the return from exile the synagogue increased in importance. It became a center of worship and education. Scholars estimate that by A.D. 69, when Jerusalem was destroyed [*sic*], no less than 400 synagogues were functioning in the city, and they were scattered in equal profusion throughout Palestine.[5]

Formal education among the Jews was rare before the exile but was common afterward. "Facilities for formal schooling practically did not exist before the Babylonian captivity."[6] Rigorous formal education then became very important to the Jews. "This provision for a higher education was probably made shortly after the return of Ezra by the rebuilding of the Temple and the foundation of synagogues. These latter institutions were originally not places of worship, but of religious instruction."[7]

By the time of Christ, boys between the ages of six and ten attended a basic grammar school in the synagogue, taught by an officer of the synagogue. Afterward the older boys would study the oral law in order to become a son of the law. When they completed this course, gifted boys from wealthy families went on to the school of a scribe, where advanced teachers such as Gamaliel, Hillel, or Shammai taught. The apostle Paul was the most famous student of Gamaliel.[8]

"In the second century before Christ the public elementary school began to grow up, and in the end became the most prominent feature of the Jewish education."[9] Such education was compulsory in Jerusalem by 75 B.C., and this requirement extended throughout all towns among the Jews by A.D. 64.[10]

The fact that human nature, especially human nature in the classroom, has not really changed over the centuries can be seen in the Talmud's categorization of four different kinds of students. First, the sponge absorbs everything. Then there is the funnel, which absorbs nothing. The third is the sieve, which catches the illustration, but misses the point. And last is the winnow, which blows away the illustrations, but gets the point.[11]

The reason why this Hebraic background for education is important for a history of Christian education should be obvious. In the first century, every synagogue had a school attached to it. Since we know that Nazareth had a synagogue, it is highly likely that Jesus attended such a school. The probability is also strong that all the apostles were educated in this way, and we know that the apostle Paul was educated within this system. Paul, who had sat at the feet of Gamaliel, was the most explicit of the apostles on the need to establish a distinctively Christian form of education, a Christian *paideia*. His urgency was not ignored. As we have seen, early Christians such as Clement of Rome promoted a *paideia* of God.

But at the same time, the Christian faith was persecuted with some regularity over the course of the first few centuries. It is hard to build institutions of learning when you are on the run. Nevertheless, by "the fourth century Christianity had developed many schools, infiltrated ancient Roman schools, and was beginning to think in terms of an educational system. Theory and methodology were being discussed in many quarters."[12] But as soon as the persecutions ceased, and the Christians found themselves in a position of influence and authority, the problem of educational institutions presented itself immediately. Classical pagan schools were still around, but Christians wanted something better. Cassiodorus wanted to "find a safe and easy equivalent to classical schools."[13] His important position in the history of education should be noted in detail.

A notable case of the kind, which deserves attention before we go on to consider the more typical educational features of monasticism, is that of Cassiodorus, who was born in South Italy sometime about 480. The greater part of his life was spent as a statesman in the service of the enlightened Ostro-Gothic kings who ruled Italy in the opening decades of the Sixth Century. Towards the end of his political career he planned to establish a Christian school in Rome in which public teachers would combine instruction in sacred literature with a training in the liberal arts. But his scheme was frustrated by the outbreak of war, and a few years later (about 540) he withdrew from the world and established two monasteries. Once again his thoughts turned to education. In addition to certain commentaries on the Scriptures, he compiled for the benefit of his monks a treatise entitled *Institutiones divinarum et saecularum lectionum*, the first part of which was devoted to sacred literature, the second to the liberal arts. The idea that all secular knowledge was comprehended in seven arts had found expression in the treatise of Martianus Capella, but the pagan atmosphere of Capella's books had prevented its general adoption. The work of Cassiodorus emphasized afresh the sevenfold grouping of knowledge and gave it sanctity by connecting it with the text that "Wisdom hath builded her house, she hath hewn out her seven pillars." Henceforward the seven arts constituted a standard part of education, and the work of Cassiodorus, unoriginal compendium as it was, became one of the texts commonly studied.[14]

So it is to Cassiodorus primarily that we owe the organization of these educational elements into seven areas.[15] Another writer notes his great contribution:

> But Cassiodorus was not merely a writer of schoolbooks; he was the founder of a monastic school, which, for the variety of sciences which it cultivated, has not infrequently been given the title of a university. And indeed it was not undeserving of the name . . . at the age of eighty-three, he undertook the composition of his treatise *De Orthographia*. He drew up a plan of studies for his scholars, and wrote for their use two treatises: "On the Teaching of Sacred Letters," and the other "On the Seven Liberal Arts." This latter was a kind of encyclopedia, including separate treatises on each subject, which formed some of the favorite elementary class-books in use during the middle ages.[16]

This was a time when Christian thinkers wrestled with the problems that came with trying to use classical learning in a Christian context. Earlier Tertullian had asked his famous question: "What does Jerusalem have to do with Athens?" Several centuries later, Christians were still working on the problem. Augustine's famous book *On Christian Doctrine* was written in part to address the problem. Augustine rejected pagan contamination. He said, "the disciplines of the pagans are unclean, because there is no wisdom in those who do not have faith."[17] And of course Cassiodorus did not want to track paganism and unbelief into the church.

> Cassiodorus was a product of an age that wavered about the reputation of the classics to promote good and foment evil. Classical authors could sometimes be tolerated, and Christian spokesmen showed some tendency to justify the liberal arts for students who had an imperative need

for them; yet it was always better to be safe than sorry, so a more cautious course of avoidance was usually followed.[18]

A common image was that of plundering gold from the Egyptians, an image used to this day. Another metaphor, and more striking, was the picture of the beautiful captive woman recorded in the book of Deuteronomy. One writer named Sidonius Apollinaris used this image to good effect—a pagan woman captured in battle could be taken as a wife, but only if she spent a month mourning her father and mother (the culture she had left forever) and if she pared her nails and shaved her head. "Philosophy was violently removed from the number of the sacrilegious arts. The hair of unnecessary religion was shorn, together with the eyebrows of secular knowledge."[19]

Rupert of Deutz put it this way: "Therefore the seven liberal arts, like maidservants, have entered into the sacred and venerable dining-room of their mistress, wisdom, and they have been redeployed, as it were, from the lawless crossroads to the strict and severe superintendence of the word of God and they have been bidden to sit down."[20] The liberal arts have abandoned their previous promiscuity, have been brought into the household of wisdom, and are now chaste.

Moreover, the content of the study could be correlated with Scripture, but one had to be wise in how it was done. "Everything that writers on the liberal arts have placed in the precincts of their own gardens can be found to some extent in the exceedingly broad meadows of Sacred Scripture. . . . They are to be ascertained in the deep roots, not in the falling leaves."[21]

And this is the origin of the Trivium, the first three of the seven liberal arts, and the Quadrivium, the last four. The Trivium was made up of grammar, dialectic, and rhetoric, while the Quadrivium was made up of arithmetic, geometry, music, and astronomy. But we have to be careful because the subjects studied were broader than their names might indicate to us today.[22]

I pass over the middle of the medieval period with some reluctance, but the educational reforms of men such as Alfred the Great in England and Charlemagne on the continent are still worth noting. "The great monarch [Charlemagne], however, even before becoming emperor, had realized that a genuine unity of his people could be brought about only through the inner life by means of a common language, culture, and set of ideas. To produce this, he felt that a revival of learning was necessary."[23]

In the late medieval period, the name of one educational reformer stands out. He is Gerhard Groote, founder of the Brethren of the Common Life. As is the case with every aspect of life in this fallen world, any tradition can become moribund when handed down lifelessly, and medieval education was no exception. Petrarch commented acidly on the state of the universities in his day (1304-1374). "The youth ascends the platform mumbling nobody knows what. The elders applaud, the bells ring, the trumpets blare, the degree is conferred, and he descends a wise man who went up a fool."[24]

The schools founded by the Brethren of the Common Life had an enormous impact on the late medieval period and were in an important sense the nursery of the Reformation. Many of the Reformers graduated from these schools, which had been established in the centuries just before the Reformation. Moreover, these schools energized classical education again.

Gerhard Groote (1340-1384) was prohibited from preaching, and so he turned to education. He was a fierce denouncer of the sins of the age. He lived to preside over the first few days of the Brethren of Common Life.[25] The schools began with a strong emphasis on morals, but their emphasis soon expanded. The Brethren "retained their Christian training, but added the classic literature and Hebrew."[26]

> The Brethren had in the first instance no special interest in humanistic studies. With such men as Geert Groote and Thomas à Kempis, the main concern was with morals and religion. But the openness of mind which showed itself in the peculiar constitution of the brotherhood made their successors ready to welcome new ideas and permit their teachers (who were not necessarily members of the Order) to adopt a curriculum of studies approximating to that which found favor in the best Italian schools.[27]

The schools had a significant impact initially, but they also had to wait until the universities shaped up enough to supply them with capable teachers. There is, incidentally, an important lesson here for classical Christian educators today. Classical education at the college level is essential to the long-term success of the classical Christian school movement at the lower levels.

> The spread of the schools of the Brethren of the Common Life throughout Germany helped to prepare the way for a general improvement of education. But it was not till the universities were able to provide a sufficient supply of well-educated teachers that the schools began to come into line with the wider movement.[28]

When we read the following description of such schools, their similarity with what we want classical Christian schools to become today should be obvious. Nothing is new under the sun.

> The curriculum was practical, emphasizing especially grammar, rhetoric, logic, ethics, and philosophy, subjects which had meaning for the life the boys would lead. The school laid great emphasis upon religion, both the Old and New Testaments, prayers, lives of saints and other religious leaders, and practical use of Christian principles.[29]

In the medieval period, the claims of Christ were understood by many to be total. For example, Anselm of Canterbury put it well when he said that the "Christian ought to advance to knowledge through faith, not come to faith through knowledge." He also said, "The proper order demands that we believe the deep things of the Christian faith before we presume to reason about them."[30] This glad acceptance of the complete authority of Christ is one of the most striking things about the intellectual life of the medieval period. Faith was not added on to the life of the mind; it was the only possible foundation for the life of the mind.

At the time of the Reformation, one great reformer in education was a Moravian bishop named John Amos Comenius. Through his work, Comenius had tremendous influence for both good and ill. The detrimental influence he exerted was because of the utopian emphasis he placed on education: "For if all men were to learn all things in all ways, all men would be wise, and the world would be full of order, light and peace."[31] In this respect he resembled the later American reformers such as Mann and Dewey. We see this belief also in the current publisher of his work—UNESCO. At the same time, in his defense, he was a sincere

Christian and would probably be appalled at what has happened in the world of education since his time.

Comenius was a shrewd man and knew what education in the classroom should be—and what an education was *for*. He put it this way: "'What madness it is,' says Seneca, 'to learn so much trash, when time is so precious.' Nothing, therefore, should be learned solely for its value at school, but for its use in life, that the information which a scholar has acquired may not vanish as soon as he leaves school."[32]

We see here a return to what we might call the comprehensiveness of a *paideia*. "Education, according to Comenius, is not merely the training of the child at school or in the home; it is a process affecting man's whole life and the countless social adjustments he must make."[33] Education is for *life*. It cannot be limited to book learning, and it is not restricted to the hours between eight and three. As such, we would add, it is inescapably religious.

One of the important things we owe to Comenius is the systematic development of a natural gradation in the curriculum. This is of special interest to classical educators who are following Sayers in her application of the Trivium to the stages of child development. Such things are obvious to us but have not always been obvious to everyone.

> If the reader wishes to realise with any force to what extent the gradation and proper articulation of studies was neglected, or rather unthought of, when Comenius was writing, let him read a few chapters in the *Great Didactic* and then turn to Milton's tractate *Of Education*. In the one he will find a rigorous distribution of the subject-matter of instruction, based on an analysis of the capacity and age of the scholar and on a common-sense estimate of the difficulty of the subject. In the other he meets with breadth of mind, it is true, but with no scheme of gradation whatever.[34]

The Reformation was not primarily an educational reformation, but education was hardly peripheral to its concerns. We have already noted the dependence of the movement on the earlier educational reforms established by the Brethren of the Common Life, but the Reformation in its turn gave great impetus to educational development. The reformers especially placed a great emphasis on classical education. This emphasis continued among Protestants down to the rise of government education in the United States, and we are just now coming back to it.

Luther did not have a high view of many of the educational institutions of his time:

> Is it not evident that it is now possible to educate a boy in three years so that when he is fifteen or eighteen years old, he shall know more than the whole sum of knowledge of the high schools and monasteries up to this time? Hitherto, in the high schools, and monasteries, men have only learned to be asses, blocks, and stones.[35]

Luther was by no means opposed to the pursuit of high educational standards. Keatinge observes: "Good schools, and nothing else, could remove monkish ignorance from the land; and this truth Luther was not slow to enunciate."[36] But of course Luther had no patience with non-Christian forms of education. "Where the Holy Scriptures are not the rule," he said, "I should advise no one to send his child."[37]

Luther's colleague Philip Melanchthon had similar views about education. "Of what importance it is to Christ's church," he says, "that boys be rightly instructed in grammar! . . . How many grievous errors I might relate that have wrought great havoc in the Church, and that have arisen solely from ignorance of grammar!"[38]

The Calvinistic wing of the Reformation was no different, and the emphasis again was on rigorous classical study:

> But though the religious side of education was prominent in all Calvin's plans, he also saw the need for a secular education. "Although we accord the first place to the Word of God," he said in a prospectus of the elementary schools written by him in conjunction with his old teacher, Mathurin Cordier, who had come to Geneva to lend his aid in school work, "we do not reject good training. The Word of God is indeed the foundation of all learning, but the liberal arts are aids to the full knowledge of the Word and not to be despised."[39]

Calvin founded schools and promoted education, so much so that the city of Geneva took the lead in promoting learning throughout Europe. Schools "of the Calvinist type rapidly spread among the Huguenots of France, who by this means soon became far better educated than the rest of their countrymen."[40]

John Knox, the fiery Scot, spent time in Geneva, and he brought the Calvinistic emphasis back to Scotland. Contrary to popular misunder-

standings of Knox, he was one of the most enlightened and progressive
leaders of his day, particularly in the realm of education. We might not
be able to judge from his spelling, but he placed a great value on thorough education: "Of necessitie we judge it, that everie severall Churche
have a schoolmaister appointed, suche a one as is able, at least, to teache
Grammar and the Latine toung, yf the Toun be of any reputation."[41]

Scotland was the most Calvinistic of all the nations of Europe, and
the leaders of the Reformation there were dedicated to the reform of
education.

> Immediately on the adoption of the Confession of Faith and the sever-
> ance of the Church from Rome by the Act of the Scottish Parliament
> in 1560, he [Knox] and four other ministers prepared the remarkable
> First Book of Discipline as the basis of the national Church polity. An
> essential part of the scheme was a system of educational institutions
> under Church control for all classes of the community, which for
> breadth and comprehensiveness has no peer among the educational
> proposals of this period.[42]

The Puritans in England to the south continued this glorious tradition. "Not only were the existing schools carefully conserved in the
midst of violent ecclesiastical changes, but a considerable number of new
schools were established in Wales and the north of England under two
Acts for the Propagation of the Gospel."[43] And it has to be emphasized
that this education was rigorously Christian—and classical. "Wherever
the Calvinists went, from Transylvania to Massachusetts, they brought
with them not only the Bible and Calvin's *Institutes*, but the Latin grammar and the study of the classics."[44]

Of course, this was a period in the history of the West when a good
portion of the West decided to move . . . west. This was due to many
factors—curiosity, flight from persecution, desire to establish a genuine
Christian commonwealth, and desire to make money. But for whatever
reason, enormous numbers of Reformed Protestants came to the New
World, and they brought their classical forms of Christian education
with them. The historian Samuel Morison notes the interrelatedness
of Puritanism and classical study: "The classics flourished in New
England under Puritanism, and began to decay when Puritanism with-
ered." This Puritanism was interested in the world and pursued edu-

cation as a way of glorifying God. "Puritanism was unascetic; it came to terms with this world."[45]

Now we come to the great change that took place in education as our modern innovators came along to suggest that we depart from a long and honored tradition. They were successful with their agenda, for the most part, but we now must seriously consider how deep the failure of their form of education has been. In the classical Christian school resurgence, we are being called to return to a repentant understanding of our own history. Christopher Dawson's insights on our failure are so profound that it is worthwhile to quote him extensively as we consider where we are on the timeline of educational reformations.

> For the educated person cannot play his full part in modern life unless he has a clear sense of the nature and achievements of Christian culture: how Western civilization became Christian and how far it is Christian today and in what ways it has ceased to be Christian: in short, a knowledge of our Christian roots and of the abiding Christian elements in Western culture.[46]

The contents of this chapter should make this obvious, but I need to make the point anyway: I differ decidedly with Dawson's Roman Catholicism but have no problem embracing his catholicity.

Those who are laboring for a recovery of true education in our day can feel lonely at times. Some feel lonely all the time. But it has always been this way. Lonely education reformers are part of a great host. *Many* have been in this situation before us.

> Indeed, every advance in education has been prepared by a preliminary period in which the pioneers work outside the recognized academic cadres. This was so at the beginning of the European university and in the beginnings of humanism, while today the diffusion of leisure throughout the affluent society offers new opportunities for free intellectual activity.[47]

In other words, we are not in an unusual position in this regard. But we do have one great advantage over our fathers—the Jews coming back from exile in Babylon, the fathers combating paganism, the Brethren establishing medieval schools, the Reformers continuing their great work—and that advantage is obvious when we think about it.

Comparatively speaking, we are rich. Our fathers did far more with much less. But we need not continue to lag behind.

There is no return to the culture of the West without a return to the historic Christian faith.

> Behind the existing unity of Western culture we have the older unity of Christian culture which is the historic basis of our civilization. . . . Even after the unity of Christendom had been broken by the Reformation, the traditions of Christian culture still survived in the culture and institutions of different European peoples.[48]

Many eulogies have been spoken over Western civilization, but in my view they are all premature. The West is far more resilient than many suppose, but at the same time we cannot presume that traditions can last forever without a defense—a defense that is self-consciously articulated. Dawson maintains: "We must make an effort to achieve an open Christian culture which is sufficiently conscious of the value of its own tradition to be able to meet secularist culture on equal footing."[49]

We need to turn around and look back over the centuries. In our nation, we face many challenges as we seek to faithfully teach our children in the light of the Gospel of Jesus Christ. But such challenges are nothing new. We have conquered many such adversaries before this, and our children will have to conquer many more. So we look forward to the establishment of a second Christendom, inspired by what it took to establish the first.

> Christendom, the historic reality of Christian culture as a world movement, was created by the conversion of Hellenistic Roman culture to Christianity and its diffusion to the peoples of the West. To use my terminology, it was a "superculture" which absorbed and overlaid a large number of cultures of various degrees of importance. In the course of ages it has passed through many phases and influenced the development of many different peoples. It has inherited the sacred learning of the Hebrews and the wisdom of the Greeks and the law of the Romans and has united them in a new unity. It has created new spiritual ideals and new philosophies and new arts and new social institutions. But throughout the course of its history, it has preserved the unity of the Christian faith and the community of the Christian people. Christian education today is the bearer of this millennial tra-

dition and possesses all the treasures of three thousand years of spiritual creativity.[50]

And this is why we remain confident. "So long as the Christian tradition of higher education still exists, the victory of secularism even in a modern technological society is not complete. There is still a voice to bear witness to the existence of the forgotten world of spiritual reality in which man has his true being."[51]

There remains a witness for the people of God. There is a bumper sticker that says, "If you can read this, thank a teacher." But we should say that if you can read a chapter such as this and understand the heritage we have, thank God for three millennia of teachers.

15

THE TRIVIUM

DEPENDING ON THE PERSPECTIVE of the one observing, the word *classical* can have either good or bad connotations. Few respond to it with an apathetic shrug. But either way, what does classical education have to do with the Christian faith? Despite the long history of the connection between the Christian faith and classical education, as presented in the last chapter, it is still very easy for conservative modern Christians (especially Americans) to dismiss all that as one long history of compromise. The American church has a relatively short history of assuming that true Christianity disappeared when the last apostle died and did not reappear until the camp meetings on the Kentucky frontier in 1799. Some, more moderate in their views, do not think the church disappeared until the third or fourth century, but it always seems to reappear just in time to authenticate *our* forms of worship and doctrine. This restorationist approach to church history trains us to view virtually all developments within church history with a jaundiced eye. We tend to identify with Tertullian's famous question, "What does Jerusalem have to do with Athens?" Thus we tend to be suspicious of things such as the Trivium.

But others say that the Trivium is morally neutral and so is just fine as far as it goes. But this still removes a scriptural motivation for pursuing it in education. So should we not just dismiss any controversy over this question as a "secular" pedagogical issue? But we cannot do this if we have understood what is meant by approaching *all* things, education included, in the light of Scripture. Classical Christian educators want to acknowledge the lordship of Christ in every subject they teach in their schools, but surely they cannot exempt their own pedagogical studies. The authority of Scripture must include any classes in which future teachers are taught. So in what ways can we argue that our approach to education in the Trivium is consistent with Scripture?

First, what do we mean by classical? As much as we might be tired of the question, to repeat the same things again is no trouble to me, and is helpful for others (Phil. 3:1). Misunderstanding of the word *classical* is forgivable because the world has been going on for a long time, and many things have become classic simply because of their antiquity. There are numerous competing definitions, mentioned earlier. So the only thing we can do is simply stipulate how *we* are using the word. Such a stipulation includes two basic things—the methodology of the Trivium and the heritage of Western civilization. I'm not saying that this is the only legitimate definition of classical education; the stipulation is simply made for the sake of accuracy and clarity in communication. Of course, in the Christian approach to this matter, we cannot simply stipulate what we mean, but we must also go on to see how the stipulated definitions line up with Scripture.

The Trivium refers to the first three of the seven liberal arts and consists of grammar, dialectic, and rhetoric. Just as the word *classical* expands out in many directions, so does the word *Trivium*. Within the Trivium, the constituent parts are enormous subjects in their own right. With regard to educational pedagogy, our definitions of these terms are stipulated as well.

Grammar is not simply linguistic, but should be understood as the constituent parts of each subject. In the study of language, of course, grammar has to do with verbs, nouns, direct objects, and the occasional exclamation. But math has a grammar as well, as does geography. The grammar of math would be the addition tables and subtraction tables. In geography the grammar would be rivers, towns, continents, and mountain ranges. The grammar of history would be timelines, names, dates, and battles. But someone may have taken all sorts of these facts on board and still not be educated. The vision of a precocious fifth grader comes to mind. The Lord High Executioner in *The Mikado* was aware of this kind of kid—the "child who is up on dates, and floors you with them flat." Knowledge of grammar alone equips someone to play games of Trivial Pursuit but not much else. At the same time, attempting to go on to the other levels of the Trivium without this foundation is also disastrous.

Dialectic can also be referred to as logic. After a child has memorized piles of data, he or she must learn how to sort them out. Dialectic, or logic, is the process of doing this—this goes over here, and that goes there.

The study of rhetoric, according to Quintilian, concerns the art of a good man speaking well. In the educational context, rhetoric concerns how the students present what they have learned. How do they communicate it? Polish without substance is sophistry. Substance without polish is . . . well, actually we don't know what it is because nobody pays attention to it.

This view of the Trivium assumes the course of study to be chronological. First we have grammar—the accumulation of factoids. Then comes dialectic—the sorting out of facts into truth and goodness. Then rhetoric is the presentation of that truth and goodness in a lovely form.

Now how are we to understand the Trivium in the light of Scripture? Where do we start? All things must start with a healthy fear of God. "The fear of the LORD is the beginning of knowledge, but fools despise wisdom and instruction" (Prov. 1:7). If we begin with ourselves or with ancient teachers, we will always stumble and fall. If we do not ground everything we do on the teaching of Scripture, our compromise will at some point undo us. Many Christians are understandably nervous about taking any kind of "gold from the Egyptians" because we are aware that many unbelieving practices contain within them unbelieving but hidden assumptions. If Christians imitate those practices, they may find themselves unwittingly embracing the underlying assumptions.

At the same time, we are not required to believe the opposite of whatever any unbeliever discovers. Through common grace, many unbelievers have noticed that the sky is blue and that canaries are yellow. This is fine, and faithfulness does not require any hot denials from us. However, the fact that unbelievers think that the yellow canary is actually a distant cousin of the brown moose is *not* the result of common grace, but is rather the result of some strange and very unscientific investigations.

If we want to know how to maintain the proper distinctions, we have to ground our approach to the Trivium in Scripture. The wisdom literature of Scripture gives us certain distinctions that apply to our subject, referring to knowledge, understanding, and wisdom. *Knowledge* corresponds to grammar. *Understanding* corresponds to dialectic, and *wisdom*—just like rhetoric—is the capstone of all the previous study.[1]

Throughout Scripture, we regularly see these three words distinguished, sometimes in the same passage. "For the LORD giveth wisdom; out of his mouth cometh knowledge and understanding" (Prov. 2:6; *cf.* Ex. 35:35). The point here is not to draw an exact mathematical correlation between these distinctions and the classical terminology. At the same time, the similarities are remarkable—so remarkable that it is clear that we are talking about the same basic things.

In the wisdom literature of Scripture, knowledge corresponds with grammar. "Cease to hear instruction, my son, and you will stray from the words of knowledge" (Prov. 19:27 ESV). In Scripture, knowledge is connected with hearing (or refusing to hear) specific words of instruction. A fool does not want to be bothered. One who is diligent to hear will come eventually to wisdom. In the classical method, grammar refers to the body of information that must be taken in by the student, information given at the beginning of the course of instruction. Grammar is the simple inculcation of the facts of the case, and the youngest student can grasp this.

In a similar way, understanding corresponds to dialectic. "The fear of the LORD is the beginning of wisdom: a good understanding have all they that do his commandments" (Ps. 111:10). Notice that in Scripture, *understanding* has a strong ethical component. Now a scriptural approach to ethics emphasizes discernment—that is, *this* and not *that*. In the classical method, dialectic refers to the practice of sorting out and relating all the knowledge that has been, and is being, accumulated. "This goes here, and that goes there." At this point, all Christian educators must know that *clear thinking is a moral issue*. Blurry thinking is one of the great sins of the age. To teach the dialectical stage without a constant grounding in the ethical absolutes of Scripture is worse than folly. Learning to distinguish rightly, learning to evaluate, is the meaning of holiness. As we seek to understand the world around us, we are seeking understanding in this biblical sense.

In a Christian school, discernment should be at the center of teaching at the dialectic stage. During this time, the students should be learning, in brief, who the good guys are and who the bad guys are. Who is right, and who is wrong? Dialectic does not refer simply to the making of distinctions, but to the evaluation of those distinctions. To see that a horse is not a duck belongs to the grammar stage. To see that a horse is a suitable animal to use in battle, and that a duck is not, belongs to the dialectic stage.

Wisdom corresponds to rhetoric. "The tongue of the wise useth knowledge aright: but the mouth of fools poureth out foolishness" (Prov. 15:2). Notice that wisdom has to do with the right use of knowledge. A young woman can be given knowledge and can be called knowledgeable. But we would not necessarily say that such a student, however good she might be at chattering facts, is wise. Children can memorize stacks of data, but this is not wisdom. This kind of knowledge, if it does not acquire the ballast of obedient wisdom, "puffs up" its owner. In Scripture, wisdom refers to the arrangement and application of knowledge and understanding. The exercise of wisdom will of course lead to more knowledge and understanding, which will in its turn be arranged. Wisdom answers the question of how to present or apply knowledge.

Not surprisingly, in the classical method rhetoric is essentially the same thing. A person who was quick with words was not someone "good at rhetoric." We return to Quintilian's definition of rhetoric as a good man speaking well. In a Christian context, good is defined by Scripture. Just as a person cannot be wise without being good, so a person cannot be a rhetorician in the biblical sense without being good.

All that remains is the application to the various ages of child development. In Dorothy Sayers's seminal essay, "The Lost Tools of Learning," she argued that there was a precise correspondence between the elements of the Trivium and certain stages of child development. When we first established Logos School, we took her word for it, as it all seemed to make good sense. But in the twenty years since, we have seen this insight tested and proven time and again. Sayers offered us a remarkable pedagogical insight, and the ramifications for the education of our children are profound. The stages of development are discussed below.

Poll-parrot. At this stage children love to chant, memorize, and recite. When they want to take on data, we have them take on data. Most modern educators stumble at this point because of their antipathy to "rote learning." They are chronologically troubled over nothing. Rote learning is a poor substitute for education when it is applied at the wrong place. But when accumulation of facts is a joy and a delight to a child, and quite a bit of it has to be done in any case, why not do it here? In the American educational system, this stage is (roughly speaking) the elementary years—starting to taper off in sixth grade.

Pert. This is generally the junior high years. Kids become inquisitive and disputatious. As Sayers argues, when they want to argue, teach them how to argue. This is the age when they want to know why and, furthermore, how come? The Sayers insight for all ages could be summed up this way: *Teach with the grain.* So we teach formal symbolic logic to our eighth graders, along with other dialectical study such as formal grammar.

Poetic. At this time of life, children are concerned with appearances. If we have grasped the principle, then we teach them how to present themselves. Consequently, here we would locate the literature courses, the rhetoric course, the apologetics course, and so on. These are the high school years. The reason we have so many "undisciplined" kids trying so hard to be "cool" is not because they are slovenly or lazy. They are trying hard to "present" but have not been taught how to do so. The result is various, disheveled "rhetorics": "Dude, like I was totally *there.*"

We are in the wonderful position of having discovered something that is profoundly effective. We should master the principles (*not* methods) and seek to make as many applications as we may. In so doing, we are following the same (general) chronological order with the terms found in Scripture. Knowledge is given to young children. They are told to seek understanding. If they seek understanding diligently, over time they will come into wisdom.

The second important aspect of classical and Christian education has to do with the *content* of what is taught. Why do we emphasize the history of Western civilization? Why is there an emphasis on Latin? Couldn't the method outlined above—grammar, dialectic, and rhetoric—be somehow applied in a school for VCR repairmen? How does the content matter?

We must recover a doctrine of history. In the providence of God, the kingdom of God was preached in the Greco-Roman world, and Christianity spread, for the most part, north and west. The direction of this movement has changed recently but only in the last century or so. Now the kingdom of God *is not to be identified with Western culture*, but we must say at the same time that the stories of each are so intertwined that we cannot hope to understand the course of one without knowing the history of the other. So to Christian educators Constantine and Charlemagne will always be more significant than the Ming Dynasty. The course of history was established by a sovereign God, and we teach this history to our children as a form of submission to Him.

We must also recover a doctrine of generations: Our children *grow*. They do not grow up in a detached way, as though the twig were unrelated to the branch, which in turn is unrelated to the tree. Our children are not interchangeable ball bearings, able to be placed in different machines across the world; they are olive shoots around *our* tables. In our individualistic times, we tend to think of previous generations or eras as though they were a series of ponds. We used to live around a pond that everyone called "the fifties." Then later we lived around another pond called "the nineties." But this is not how the Bible encourages us to think about history at all. History is a river, and we live downstream from our ancestors and upstream from our descendants. This means, in turn, that we have to educate particular children, dealing with the particular languages, battles, dates, nations, and people. And our schools must spend a good deal of time talking about Constantine, Charlemagne, Charles Martel, John Knox, and George Washington.

Putting it together, we seek to establish our children in knowledge, understanding, and wisdom. Using pedagogical terms, we educate them in grammar, dialectic, and rhetoric. They should be brought to know the truth, understand the good, and attain wisdom in that which is lovely.

16

A CASE FOR LATIN

ONE OF THE MOST common questions classical educators face is this natural one: "Why Latin?" In our postmodern times, it might be tempting for us to shrug and ask, "Why not?" But we should probably do better than this. At the crossroads of life, it appears that we always have to give a reason for going right instead of left. If we drop our dress code requirements, virtually no one wants to know why. But if we tighten those same requirements, we had better have all our reasons lined up in a row. Few have to give a reason for lowering the bar. Reasons are always necessary for raising it.

Therefore, we have to give reasons for adding a Latin requirement or for keeping our Latin requirements in our schools. We can accept this demand with a recognition that there is a way of returning to the "old paths" that arouses justified suspicions. The questions can be reasonable. "To proclaim the salutary nature of tradition, and in particular the possibility of conversation with the past, is not the same as traditionalism, which is the assertion of one sector of time, the past, against the present."[1] In arguing for a return to the disciplined study of Latin, we do not do so mindlessly, simply because Latin is old. Some things improve with age, like wine, but other things do not, like pizza. I want to argue that Latin is in the former category.

Near the beginning of the twentieth century, Francis Kelsey gave a detailed list of reasons urging the study of Latin and Greek, but I want to reduce his list to four general categories: The study of Latin promotes mental discipline; it encourages literary appreciation; it leads to a mastery of English; it provides a solid foundation for preparation for Christian ministry.[2]

The first reason is the need for mental discipline. Latin is a more precise language than English, and the exercise of learning what the different case endings do (for just one example) encourages precision of thought. A good education encourages such attention to detail in all things but especially in language. The reason mental discipline is difficult is that we live in a fallen world, and God has cursed the ground so that thorns and thistles grow there. Laziness and sin both make people want to coast downhill; Chesterton once said that Satan fell by the force of gravity. We like to relax our Latin standards for the same reason that we prefer riding our bicycles downhill as opposed to uphill. Work is hard, but it is also profitable. "Whatever the grievances of the past, present attacks on the classics are inspired by the revolt against discipline and hard work, the impatience of all serious pre-vocational study, the demand for quick utilitarian results, and absorption in the up-to-date."[3]

These comments were published in 1911. It is difficult to imagine what the writer would say today if he had the opportunity to confront our instant mind-set where students want to get all their multicultural experiences out of a can, ready to be heated up in the microwave.

But hard work and precision are not ends in themselves. When we learn the importance of intellectual discipline, we can soon relate the value of that discipline to other tasks and from that point to the ultimate goal, which is the glory of God. So I would like to argue that the brain is a muscle, not a shoebox. And I would also like to hasten to explain myself.

If a football coach were making his player run wind sprints in a particularly hard practice, no one would upbraid him for making his players run from the thirty-yard line to the forty-yard line and then, mindlessly, pointlessly, back again. If he were confronted, he would point out that the issue was discipline and not the particular piece of ground the players were covering. In fact the ground covered in the subsequent game is not important in itself either but is related to a higher end.

We tend to think of our students' minds as finite shoeboxes, and we then think we must take special care not to put anything in there if we do not want it to remain there for life. But the brain is more like a muscle. A student who learns one language, such as Latin, is not stuck with his shoebox three-quarters full, with no room for Spanish. Rather the student has a mind that has been stretched and exercised in such a way that subsequent learning is much easier, not much harder.

Now of course this kind of mental discipline *could* be acquired by requiring of the students the intellectual equivalent of running back and forth. While a football coach might be able to get away with this, because everyone understands the point, we should not attempt it in the classroom—although mental wind sprints that had no point in themselves would still be better than simple laziness. The reason this approach would not work in the classroom is that the human mind is inescapably teleological; it wants to know why it is learning something. Latin has the advantage of providing the grist for the mill of the mind, while also providing great practical advantages. To return to our metaphor of football, the study of Latin is therefore simultaneously an exercise to prepare for the game *and* part of the game.

Incidentally, before we leave this point, it should be noted that mental slackness, especially in institutions, is contagious. Once the standards start to slip, they slide across the board, culture-wide, and it becomes increasingly difficult for *anyone* to maintain the higher standards. "The down drag of a low ideal, when it exists throughout a vast body of men, is a very powerful force and one which is extremely difficult to counteract."[4] The natural tendency is always *down*. "The tendency, as I believe, of those who do not possess these weapons of a full Christian culture must ever be to read what is easier."[5] If we do not reverse this tendency in the early years, I am afraid we will not be able to reverse it at all.

Long experience has shown us that the discipline required for learning another language, particularly Latin, and the work of learning to translate is a discipline peculiarly suited for application elsewhere. "The critical interpretation or translation of such a language supplies the simplest and most effective all-round discipline of the greatest number of faculties."[6] The connections with the rest of life are numerous.

Our second consideration, the capacity for literary appreciation, is also important. Many great literary works—works that will be studied to the end of the world—were written in Latin. From Virgil's *Aeneid* to Augustine's *Confessions*, the Latin language has served a foundational role in world literature. Noah and his wife are more important, ancestrally speaking, than someone's great aunt in Des Moines because they are *everyone's* ancestors. In the same way, Latin is more important than Esperanto or Ebonics. Simply because of the position Latin occupies, the literature of Spain, France, England, and so on rest upon it.

The study of Latin gives advanced students the capacity to read Virgil in the original. Also they would find it easier to learn classical Greek, which works the same way Latin does, and this opens up the world of Homer and Sophocles. But even if they do not progress to the level of reading in the original, they have greater appreciation for such books, having laboriously translated portions of them and having read them in translation.

But these first two reasons may strike more pragmatic Americans as remarkably uncompelling—which is why I put them first. We do not want to live in accordance with the dictates of pragmatism, which can be hung with its own rope. *Pragmatism doesn't work.* At the same time, commitment to something more important than immediate success often has the side benefit of immediate success.

Mastery of English is directly related to success in life—whether in business, school, or elsewhere. But thorough mastery of English is dependent upon the study of Latin. About 80 percent of our English vocabulary comes from Latin and Greek, with over 50 percent coming from Latin. Students who study Latin in high school for several years can assume that it will be good for a hundred points on the verbal portion of the SAT.

> The study of Latin and Greek contributes to the student's command of English through the enlargement of his vocabulary, and the enrichment of it in synonyms expressing the finer shades of meaning; through his acquaintance with the original or underlying meaning of words, through his familiarity with the principles of word formation, and through the insight into the structure of the English language afforded by a mastery of Latin.[7]

That statement makes perfect sense. So many English words can be traced back to Latin that it would be difficult to deny that the traffic can go the other way. In other words, if someone learns the English word *constitution*, to take one example, he has learned one word. But if he learns the Latin word meaning *I stand*, which is *sto*, he learns an important component of the English words *constitution*, *institution*, and *restitution*, along with many others. If he has learned *bene*, meaning "well," and *dico*, meaning "I say," he can anticipate the meaning of *benediction*, *malediction*, *valedictory*, *dictation*, *dictator*, and more *ad nauseam*, which is also Latin. Charles R. Williams put it well: "Almost imperceptibly he finds his range of expression amplified; his appreciation of delicate shades of thought quickened; his vocabulary expanding; his ability to think more clearly and to give utterance to his thought with propriety and precision vastly augmented."[8]

Some classical purists may still object to this kind of argument, saying rightly that pragmatism doesn't work. No, but Latin does. A school that has a Latin program should not maintain it for simple pragmatic reasons, but it is still good to be able to show the cash value of such study to parents who are considering enrollment and are willing to be persuaded. They don't know about the Latin but are willing to give it a try, as long as you give them something they can take home on a brochure. Once they have been with the school for a time, the remaining benefits will have had a chance to prove themselves.

The last reason for teaching Latin is related to the fact that classical Christian schools are *Christian* schools. They are not pre-ministerial academies, but many of our future pastors are going to be graduates of these schools. Moreover, many of their parishioners will have been their classmates. A grounding in Latin will be a great benefit to the future of the church. Ministers who are well-educated, preaching to souls who are also recipients of a thoroughly Christian education, will do a great deal to raise the standard above the current happy-clappy level.

The inscription over Christ's head on the cross was written partly in Latin. Christ was born into a Latin-speaking empire. The language of intellectual discourse was still Greek, but within a few centuries Greek gave way to Latin in the western part of the Empire. Latin remained the language of the Western Christian civilization for the next millennium and a half.

Vast treasures of history and theology are tied up in the Latin tongue. This history is not limited to Roman Catholic sources. The great Puritan John Owen wrote a Latin work called *Biblical Theology*, which has just recently been translated into English. Also in recent years, the works of Francis Turretin were translated out of the Latin into English for the first time. But in the nineteenth century, R. L. Dabney had his seminary students use those works in the original Latin as textbooks. The importance of Latin was not limited to Roman Catholics or to Europeans. According to Christopher Dawson, "Latin was the language of the liturgy and the

Bible, and in the new lands it had to be acquired by men who had no immediate contact with the Latin-speaking world."[9]

The Christian ministry is not a place for intellectual slackness. William Douglas Mackenzie says:

> The Christian religion cannot possibly retain moral and social leadership if its ministers lack an intellectual equipment which is equal to that required by any calling in the most civilized regions of the world. The idea that Christianity can conquer by means of men who do not know what mental discipline is, who hope to maintain their influence by a piety that is divorced from intelligence, or a message that is delivered by intellectual incompetents, is one of the most disastrous which any generation could inherit or cherish.[10]

The twentieth century in America has seen the Christian church grow in numbers and influence. But that influence has been simply part of the pop culture scene—John 3:16 placards at football games—and has not offered any serious moral, doctrinal, or aesthetic leadership. We have not thus far had the wherewithal.

17

WHAT CLASSICAL IS NOT

WE HAVE ALREADY noted that the word *classical* can be used in various legitimate and not so legitimate ways. But my purpose in this chapter is to limit my critique of pseudo-classicism to those types within the ranks of the classical Christian school movement. As Karen Grant once put it, bright lights attract big bugs. The bright light of classical Christian education has attracted many diligent parents and teachers, and wonderful things are happening in our schools. But the movement has also attracted a few head cases, poseurs, charlatans, and bemused spectators. As the movement continues to grow, I would like to be on record concerning some of the weirder manifestations of "classical education."

But to approach this in the right way, we have to understand a basic biblical principle—the Sabbath principle. We must carefully learn how readily this principle can get twisted into something else. In the book of Deuteronomy, we come across a law that strikes modern ears as somewhat odd. The law, considered in itself, is clearly a kind one, but the occasion that gave rise to the ordinance is not one we encounter every day. Or do we? When we consider the misunderstandings regarding this law, we should discover that the more things change, the more they stay the same.

Moses required that the Israelites refrain from seething or boiling a kid in its mother's milk (Deut. 14:21). The placement of this law in Deuteronomy is right at the beginning of Moses' exposition of the fourth commandment, the Sabbath law. This insignificant law has many applications, which ostensible friends of the Sabbath need to learn. Unfortunately, it also contains a principle that has been too frequently ignored in broader contexts, including that of education. The law says that a young goat must not be cooked in its mother's milk. The principle is self-evident: *That which is intended by God to be the means of sustaining life must not be changed into an instrument of death.* In this regard, God clearly demands respect for the natural order of things.

When Paul cites a similarly kind provision for animals, i.e., that an ox treading out the grain must not be muzzled, he makes a passing comment we would do well to note: "Is it *oxen* God is concerned about?" (1 Cor. 9:9, emphasis mine). A man could woodenly obey the law and have his oxen unmuzzled—"That's what the law *says*," he mutters—and that same man could refuse to support ministers of the Gospel financially. If he were to do so, he would be disobedient to the law that speaks of oxen only. Paul applies this Old Testament law to a New Testament situation. His method is to argue his point from the usual order of things (1 Cor. 9:7) and to argue it from the *law* (v. 8). So was this law concerning baby goats a random piece of Mosaic legislation in response to diligent activity by the goat lobby? Those who think so understand neither the Scriptures nor the kindness of God.

Whenever we talk about Sabbath issues (and, rightly understood, education *is* a Sabbath issue), we have a sinful tendency to rush to all the wrong questions. "Can I do this? Do I get to do that? God's point in all this is clearly to wreck my Sunday afternoons." But the first principle is given clearly by Isaiah: Call the Sabbath a *delight* (Isa. 58:13). And even this verse is abused whenever truncated, narrow, and parsimonious Sabbath observance is substituted for the real thing. The cranky Sabbatarian, who "cooks kids in their Sabbath milk," does not limit this destructive behavior to one day in seven. This mind-set shows up in classrooms and turns what should be the kids' life—their education— into an instrument of torture and death.

Moses warned against this mind-set, and Jesus rebuked it: The Sabbath was made for man, not man for the Sabbath. The milk was for the kid, not the kid for the milk. *Think* for a moment, the Word tells us. The classroom is for the child; the child is not for the classroom. The Sabbath is a *feast*, not a fast (Lev. 23:2-3). The Lord's day is a *feast*, not a fast (Jude 12). We are to avoid corrupting a holy feast with selfishness and immorality (1 Cor. 11:20-21; Jude 12). We are also to avoid destroying this feast by throwing away all the food. We must reject all forms of pious masochism. Our God is a God who gives us a weekly holy day—that is, holiday. He urges celebration one day out of seven. He wants to be invited and honored during this rich feasting. This richness is the goodness of whole milk. But a common truncated Sabbatarianism is low-fat milk, and its adherents wonder why non-Sabbatarians hate the Sabbath!

Our gracious God has given us milk and honey in many other forms, although the sinful heart wants to twist them all. Marital love is given by God to be an expression of the closest possible union between human beings, but many make it into an occasion for tension and conflict. Marriage is an occasion to give, not to grab. Another example is women in combat. Women are designed by God to nurture and sustain life, not to be death-dealers or kinky warriorettes (Deut. 22:5). And the home is an example. There is a vast difference between home cooking and being cooked at home. What are some of the things that cause the sweet nourishment of a home to be turned into a cauldron of death? The list is clearly not exhaustive, but consider just a few: displays of temper, a critical spirit, nagging, and the long face of a pious killjoy. Because of the nature of the case, parents with a critical, nagging spirit are likely to be involved in the formation of a new school. They *hate* what is going on in the government schools. Pious killjoys love your new school too and show up on the first day.

So how does all this apply to education? We need to carefully consider the inescapable situation we are in. Either we feed and nourish the children of God, or we cook and eat them. If we love God, if we love our children, if we love our own souls, we must *consider our ways and live.* A good teacher is one who loves God, loves her students, loves her subject matter, and who communicates all three loves effectively to those students. An essential part of good teaching is loving the material in the presence of others, whom you also love. If anything less than this is happening in the classroom, *the students are being cooked rather than being fed.*

> The fault of many teachers is that they do not let their children near them, but endeavor to foster a kind of awful respect. Before you can teach children you must get the silver key of kindness to unlock their hearts, and get their attention. Say, "Come, ye children." We have known some good men who are objects of abhorrence to children.[1]

The education nazis will see this as a call to lower standards or watered-down discipline. But the concern here is the relationship of educational discipline to the children, not the presence or absence of such discipline. I have no problem with high standards or tight rules—but the rules are *for* the children; the children are not there to give the rules something to work upon. There is nothing wrong with hard work in a rigorous school, but there is something wrong with work that is hard for all the wrong reasons. Every capable teacher should be striving to make the environment of the classroom *normal* and life-giving. This kind of discipline is life; it is drinking milk, not eating gravel. Augustine put it well: "We often have to take bitter medicines, and we must always avoid sweet things that are dangerous: but what better than sweet things that give health, or medicines that are sweet?"[2] The confusion of means and ends here is easy to see. The stable stays very clean with no livestock in it. But wealth comes through the labor of an ox (Prov. 14:4).

Another related problem in classical schools, less hard on the kids but still counterproductive in the long run, is what I call school-marmishness. The "rules" for a discipline are mastered and memorized, but no one appears to know why these are studied—just *because*. Students of rhetoric learn a bunch of stuff about rhetoric, which actually means that they can pass a test on terms in rhetoric class. They still can't speak effectively, but they know the difference between the *exordium* and the *narratio*. Some teachers want students to learn about the subject, with no possible application. Or a Latin teacher demands an ability to regurgitate the rules of Latin grammar (which is fine), but no one ever really gets proficient in the language. Augustine knew of this problem long ago: "Given a sharp and eager mind, eloquence is picked up more readily by those who read and listen to the words of the eloquent than by those who follow the rules of eloquence."[3] Augustine is saying, in effect, that it would be better to learn how to play the piano by ear than to learn all kinds of music theory and not be able to play anything.

Grades are another place where this mentality reveals itself. Evaluating is necessary, but it is equally necessary to grade students in all wisdom.

Our Creator at the end of the creation week sees His work, and knowing all things infinitely, pronounces it "very good." Man, due to his sinful nature and finite knowledge, cannot evaluate perfectly. This is not a reason to avoid all evaluation but to do so with a right understanding.

When we evaluate, we must do so in light of our own deficiencies. . . .
The problem with this is that knowledge is holistic and cannot be put in
one piece at a time and left alone. Learning knowledge is learning how
to wrap string around the spool in your head. To regurgitate these facts
is like cutting a small piece of the string and coughing it on the floor.[4]

Of course every school must evaluate the students and should do so
reasonably and intelligently. But we have drifted to the point that the
grading system exists for its own sake and has to be fed at regular inter-
vals. A teacher must always remember the students, serving them with
the evaluations contained within the grade book. The students are not
to serve the needs of the grade book.

There are many cultural reasons why we fall into this confusion
about grading, many of them having to do with the lust for scientific precision that came out of the Enlightenment. Now it makes sense, for
example, if the children are taking a vocabulary test of 100 words, and
one of the kids misses thirteen of them, to give him an 87 percent. But
we go far beyond this. A student writes an essay on a sunset, let us say,
and the teacher writes 87 percent at the top of that paper. What he is saying, in effect, is that there is a mathematical metaphor operative here.
The figure of 87 is to 100 what this submitted essay is . . . to what? What
on earth is this supposed to mean?

Teachers have always evaluated students, and students have always
wanted to know how they are doing. Our problem is that we have pre-
tended that certain forms of evaluation have decimal points, and they do
not. What does it mean actually to have three credits of sociology from
a university? Can we imagine contacting John Calvin's *alma mater* and
getting a copy of his transcript? Did Gamaliel ever give Paul a B minus?

But there is always a ditch on both sides of the road. The problems
sketched above could all be grouped under the heading of strictness, irra-
tionally applied. Certain rules, laws, or systems exist for their own sake.
But the opposite problem is that of having a reputation for rigor but lacking substance. Attaching the word *classical* to the school's letterhead is
certainly easier than establishing the substance of classical education. But
there are schools, *particularly in wealthy communities*, that are able to buy
the atmosphere of classical education. Brick buildings, ivy, landscaped
grounds, high tuition, classical jargon—everything reeks of it. The prob-

lem is that in the classroom, the students are not being taught a Christian worldview, and they are not receiving a substantive classical education. Again Augustine's commentary applies: "What use is a golden key, if it cannot unlock what we want to be unlocked, and what is wrong with a wooden one, if it can, since our sole aim is to open closed doors?"[5]

Many classical Christian schools struggle against the normal kind of failure—inability to make payroll or to find a place to meet. But more than a few classical Christian schools have succumbed to the temptations of "success." The language is there, but the Christian worldview is of a scratch and sniff variety. The word *worldview* is thrown about, but it seems to mean that Christians can read and discuss foul books with impunity because they are doing it with a Christian "worldview." Here the word *worldview* is a magic charm and protects the one carrying it from the burden of having to think like a Christian. The problem is that the antithesis is being blurred. We discussed earlier the problem of maintaining a strict sense of the antithesis and putting it in the wrong place— cooking the kids instead of feeding them.

And so what we are striving for is high biblical and cultural standards—real standards—lovingly and intelligently applied. Classroom discipline in a classical Christian school should always serve as a fence to protect the students and keep them secure from those who would disrupt the process of learning. The point of discipline should never be forgotten. Discipline does not exist for its own sake.

The standards should be clear, enforced, and reasonable. When disciplinary standards meet this standard, the students know they are being respected. Such discipline, applied with wisdom, demonstrates to the students that you want them to love a subject that you also love. Refusal to discipline in a classroom setting is a refusal to protect the process of learning. Refusal to protect is tantamount to a refusal to love. And why should the students come to love a subject when they see the teacher of that subject showing contempt for it himself through his refusal to protect it? If a man were walking downtown with his wife, and suddenly she found herself being attacked by violent criminals, her husband would not have the luxury of standing off to the side wishing that this hadn't happened. We would conclude rightly that his refusal to protect her meant that he did not love her. It is the same in a classroom. A teacher who does not protect the process of learning through intelligent discipline is asking the students to show the same contempt for the subject that he does.

But then we must immediately remember the opposite error—the control freak who disciplines aimlessly. This of course is not discipline at all; it protects nothing. In fact, such discipline becomes the assailant. A classroom is a place where all behavior that disrupts the love of learning should be disciplined. Unfortunately, many gnat-strangling teachers are the principal offenders, and far from being the embodiment of biblical discipline, they should be the first recipients of it—if a wise administrator would ever sit in on the class.

18

EDUCATING THE IMAGINATION

IN THE BEGINNING, God did something. And then He did something else, and then man did something. And then the plot thickened. That is how the story started.

However, the biblical story is pretty unwieldy and remains story-like despite our best efforts. But over the course of the last 350 years, we have risen to the occasion and have trained ourselves to think of the story as just so much external baggage carrying around the internal, timeless truths. Depending on how the story is warped, we think of the timeless truths in various ways. But what matters, we think, is that invisible nugget of truth hidden deep in the recesses of the extraneous details of the story. Words carry a truth outside themselves, we think. But what truth does the story of the Incarnation "carry"? It carries nothing; it just is. Jesus said, "I *am* the truth." Truth has eight fingers and two thumbs.

The Christian imagination is not icing for the cake of education. A true understanding of the imagination is at the center of all true education. The educator must know that children, made in the image of God, love stories. But children, as sinners, seek escape as we do from the one glorious story. First, they do what unbelievers have always sought to do throughout the history of the world—tell a competing, alien story. Given the nature of the case, if they do not want to tell the story of the Creation, Fall, Incarnation, and redemption, they must in some manner seek out the story of evolution or its ancient mythological equivalents. And, incidentally, this is why the doctrine of evolution has such a grip on us. Out of all the modernist foolishness, the theory of evolution has had the staying power it does because it is a whacking good story. As C. S. Lewis put it: "It [evolution] gives us almost everything the imagination craves—irony, heroism, vastness, unity in multiplicity, and a tragic close. It appeals to every part of me except my reason."[1]

Works of imagination are not the dessert of education; they are the meal. We have to get the students to master some basic details so that they can spend their time delighting in their education. But mastering those details is not the central point. "We have to master the basics of grammar and vocabulary and figurative language before we can effectively reflect God's creative use of language. Any education that minimizes language and imagination is desperately seeking failure. Classical and Christian education delights in [language and imagination]."[2] But once the basics have been mastered, it is time to branch out into something more challenging. This approach is not a compromise with the television-based entertainment model of education; it is simply urging the older, classical approach that understood the importance of genuine imagination. As I wrote in *The Paideia of God*, "The entertainment model of education wants the students to enjoy *themselves*; the older classical model wants students to be disciplined so that they come to enjoy their *work*."[3]

The second way unbelievers try to escape God's great story is more inconsistently consistent—the attempt at the unstory, the anti-story. Just refuse to speak, hang some greasy locks in your eyes, and slouch around the place. But even this behavior is actually a rudimentary story (no getting away from the world God made), and it still gets old quickly. Nihilism is not the future. And so at some point unbelief has to revert back to some form of the counterfeit story.

We believers, in contrast, want to tell our children true stories. We are to teach them to read true stories. We should have them paint those stories and sing songs about them. The drama club should stage productions of them. Any Christian educator who wants help with such undertakings should consult the vivid Christian imagination of G. K. Chesterton. If the burden suggested by this book appears too great, he pulls us back to the right perspective: "I wish we did not have to fritter away on frivolous things, like lectures and literature, the time we might have given to serious, solid and constructive work like cutting out cardboard figures and pasting colored tinsel upon them."[4]

When children are small, we tell them Bible stories—and not in a manner that distracts from the point of the stories. We fight the war of the ages by telling the stories of all the previous battles. This rehearsal, and only this, equips students for future battles. The shape and direction of our summaries of Bible stories should faithfully follow the original. And, while we are on the subject, whatever *happened* to Bible storybooks? The stories must not be bowdlerized. What was Samson doing in Gaza in the first place? What bride-price did Saul set for Michal? And so on.

In our entertainment-crazed times, we have to take care not to use stories that have been transformed into something else. I call the process "metaphor-morphing," or "metamorphing" for short. In this process the basic metaphors of story built into the world by God are reversed. For example, the serpent in the Garden was a dragon, and it is not a coincidence that many modern stories are trying to reverse things and make the dragon out to be some sort of misunderstood soul. Always keep your eye on the dragon. This problem of metamorphing is why VeggieTales are so objectionable. King David was not a turnip, or whatever it is they have him as. The loss sustained by Christian kids who are told this stuff is incalculable. If kids learn more about the meaning of true kingship from Aragorn than they do from a story about Solomon, something is seriously distorted. But modern evangelicals are terminally irreverent. My book *Repairing the Ruins* decries this situation:

> We, the people of the Word, ought to be masters of words; Christians ought to be preeminent in wordsmithing. We are not. In this hour of crisis, we produce and sell mountains of smarmy goo and oceans of treacle. We wouldn't know a great book if it ran naked through the CBA convention.[5]

We believe that this is not irreverence because we have left the "timeless truths" inside alone. But when truths are badly adorned, or unadorned, the results are fatal. I believe further that "in a fallen world, truth cannot go out unadorned and remain what it is."[6] Truth is always incarnational. The Hellenistic/Enlightenment mind delights in disembodied truth, while the Christian faith is centered on the embodied truth. Enlightenment education always drifts to abstract rationalization.

We want to say that the externals are the externalization of the heart; they are the incarnate form of it. Without that incarnate form we have nothing.

As educators, we must come to terms with our enemy, the Enlightenment. And we really need to start calling it the Endarkenment. But, at the same time, no one should nervously imagine that this critique of the Enlightenment proceeds from any relativistic postmodern nonsense. The modernist and postmodernist share this one thing in common: They both hold, at bottom, that metaphor is meaningless. The modernist goes off to find meaning somewhere else, suitably formulaic, and the postmodernist says that everything is metaphor, and hence everything is meaningless—except for the self-awareness of the meaninglessness, but we were not expecting him to be consistent.

Often teachers in Christian schools think that they have to choose between insipid Christian literature or dangerous pagan literature. "Sometimes teachers who care about literature must feel as though they are being forced to choose between serving food prepared by a world-renowned chef, who persists in poisoning the meals, and a steady diet of *Twinkies* prepared by born-again factory workers. Is there another option?"[7]

We need to take special care to tell stories that are "not suitable" for modernists. The Bible contains dragons, giants, principalities, satyrs, and unicorns. Invariably, these get cleaned up in translation so that modernist evangelicals are not embarrassed by them. In such instances, the liberal is often to be trusted with the text of Scripture over the evangelical, because the evangelical is stuck with the results of his exegesis. If the evangelical wants to have it both ways (e.g., inerrancy *and* respectability with moderns), then he has a lot of work cut out for him. But he can rest assured that acceptance of the ancient cosmologies is *not* tantamount to belief that the earth is a flat saucer resting on the back of the primeval turtle.

We also have to tell children the history of their people. We must be careful here because we do not have the protection of inspiration. But silence does not really help because we do not have the protection of inspired silence either. We must speak or not speak as fallible persons, and the best we can do is to speak as fallible honest persons.

In our multicultural era, it is easy to represent this emphasis on

learning one's history and culture as mindless jingoism. But you cannot teach children to appreciate other cultures by teaching (by default)
contempt for your own. As I have said before, a man who dearly loves
his own mother will understand (fully) why another man regards his
mother so highly. But a man who has contempt for his own mother
will hardly rise to the occasion when someone else's mother is under
assault. The mindless nationalist has insolent pride in the history of his
country. The biblical patriot evidences affection and gratitude for his
nation.

In ascending order, the story of the region should be told and then
the story of the state. I learned the history of Maryland, but my kids grew
up learning the history of Idaho, which was entirely appropriate, albeit
somewhat shorter. Then we tell the story of the nation, fitted into the
context of the story of the civilization.

To the extent that teachers still tell stories to students, they often try
to do it in a detached, academic way. But the telling of stories *ought* to get
students worked up. The battles, after all, were yesterday. Enthusiastic
delivery leads (unfortunately, in the minds of some) to the problems created by involved storytelling. There is no neutrality. Is the storyteller
sympathetic to Lee or Grant? Is the storyteller a Tory or a Patriot?

We must also tell living stories. My father-in-law was wounded at the
battle of Guadalcanal. He has told us his war stories, and we have told
them to our children. They in turn can (and should) tell these stories to
those who come after them. Forty years from now, my sons and daughters will be in their sixties, and they can tell their grandchildren stories
about the Second World War, which they heard from their grandfather,
who was in it. To these grandchildren, World War II will seem like
ancient history. When I was a boy, I recall seeing a newspaper photo of a
reunion of men who had been in the Confederate armies. They had been
very young then, of course, but there they were.

We live our lives like fruit flies, measuring everything by the length
of our own little span, which isn't that long. We then assume that ancient
history really was a long time ago, but it was not. No doubt somewhere
in your town lives a person who is 100 years old. When that person was
a baby, she could have been placed in the lap of someone (also 100) who
was born when Thomas Jefferson was president. He in turn was born
during the reign of William and Mary. And so on. Five such lives, end to

end, take us back to the discovery of America. Five more, and we are visiting William the Conqueror. A total of twenty such lifetimes takes us back to the time of Christ. It was not that long ago.

So in your school bring in old men and women *to tell stories*. In your families, tell stories. Education is grounded upon the story we tell. That story, if it is fruitful, will inspire many other stories. If it is not, then it is just a matter of time before people decide to quit telling it.

But stories are not the only way to awaken the imagination. Children learn most naturally by imitation. In their manner of speech and walking, in their habits of thought and feeling, in their grasp of their native language, imitation is one of the foundational ways of learning. What is acquired through imitation lies close to the bone. The principle does not change with age, but it does become harder to apply because of adult pride and "settledness." Scripture observes that children are teachable, and does so while exhorting adults to be more childlike: Christians are to be imitators of God, as dear children (Eph. 5:1). In many ways, in many places, the Scriptures call disciples to a life of imitation (1 Cor. 4:15-17; 11:1; 1 Pet. 2:21; Heb. 13:7). Such imitation comes easily to children and is harder for adults, but all are called to it. Imitation occurs everywhere, but it certainly includes the use of language. "Language has always sat at the heart of classical education, and yet language is rather bizarre. Babies can use it, and yet it involves mysteries which even the most profound scholars haven't untied."[8]

> What is it about language that makes it so central? Perhaps we get some hint of this from the Incarnation itself. In the Incarnation, the invisible was made visible. The second person of the Godhead took on flesh and bone. . . . Divine imagination redraws things within language and then changes them in the material world—He calls those things which do not exist as though they did (Rom. 4:17).[9]

Now when it comes to the life of the imagination, the assumption of moderns is that creativity must spring unbidden from the artist's heart and that imitation is merely the practice of artistic hacks. But this idea owes more to the philosophy of Rousseau than to the Scriptures. A biblical aesthetic requires that true creativity be *built upon an inheritance*. Perpetual revolution is as destructive to the arts as it is to civil order. The fact that some imitate without understanding should not cause us to turn away from this approach at all. Some students struggle through math classes too, contenting themselves with the mere memorization of formulae, and they do not think about what they are learning. Nevertheless, we know that the truly creative work in mathematics is done by those who have internalized the basics; those who have grasped their inheritance can go on with it and do great things.

For a student hungry for imaginative wisdom, privileged to study with a wise master, there is no substitute for the opportunity to imitate. Imitation brings the student "up to speed," and once this happens, the mystery of God's giftedness to him then comes into play. J. R. R. Tolkien once spoke about how his creative work sprang up out of the "leaf mold of his mind." But how does that "leaf mold" get there in the first place? John Bunyan, speaking of the creative process, said that as he pulled, "it came." But *where* does "it" come from? The fact that this final mystery in creative imaginative work appears to come *ex nihilo* is only an appearance. True creativity assumes a foundation of imitation. Spurious creativity wants to pretend that no outside influences can be permitted and that the freer an artist is from such influence, the more creative the person is. But such a person (could he or she exist) would be autistic, not artistic.

Incidentally, this is one reason why all forms of cyber-education will necessarily be second best. Certain learning can be acquired at a distance, and in one sense every book ever written is a form of "distance learning." Consequently, what can be placed on a page and withdrawn from that page many years later can also be posted on the web. But the center of true education will always be flesh and blood community—first in the family and church, and then in the school or college. In community situations the powers of example and imitation display their potency.

Christian parents know that it is necessary to live out what they require of their children—but too often this is thought of as simply avoiding hypocrisy. "Do as I say, not as I do" is thought to be grounds for making a child turn away in disgust from the content of any lesson hypocritically delivered. And, of course, sometimes the truths of the Gospel are blasphemed because of hypocrisy (Rom. 2:24).

But another problem frequently arises from parental inconsistency (as well as inconsistency in teachers). Children can know and make the distinction between the message and the faults of the messenger and can be fully willing to do the right thing. *But they still do not know what the right thing looks like.* Without an incarnational model to follow, they do not know exactly what to do. "Kindness to a wife" is just a phrase, words on a page to a son who grew up in a home where kindness was not practiced. An "incarnational aesthetic" is an impossible ideal for a daughter who does not know how to adorn a table for a feast. "You iron the *napkins*?" There are many young people who are not disillusioned; they are sold on the concept, but they still do not know what to do because they have never seen it done. When children see something put into practice, they can then imitate it. When they start imitating soon enough, and if they do it long enough, they understand a behavior and internalize it. *Then* they are in a position to exercise true creativity, and what *they* do becomes worthy of imitation.

Abstractions can be true and can be affirmed, but they cannot be imitated. This is why many schools are filled with children who learn various biblical abstractions and can repeat them back, but there is nothing there to imitate. Children from other denominational traditions repeat back a different set of abstractions. The lives of the two groups of children do not differ that much from one another because you imitate what you see, not what you hear. None of the children see a distinctively Christian culture. They all see the same basic secular American culture poured through a rudimentary sieve (designed to catch the larger chunks of secularism) into the jars of differing ecclesiastical traditions. And they imitate what they see.

If we want a renaissance of the imagination in the next generation, we have to give children something to copy. If they can imitate it, they can eventually surpass it. If the process breaks down, then we will continue in this cultural quicksand.

The goal of classical education in our schools is rhetoric, broadly understood. I explained this term in *The Paideia of God*: "We need to be constantly reminded that logic and grammar are the preparation for the last level of the Trivium, that of rhetoric, the level where young men and women come to maturity, growing up to the level of understanding *poetry*."[10] We do not have them master the grammar and the dialectic so that they can chop logic for the rest of their dreary lives. They should grow up into wisdom, rhetoric, glory, and again, *poetry*.

And this brings us to the importance of music education. I have said many times that the main conduit of relativism into the church today is the realm of aesthetic issues. The main culprit is music. The music of the world gets worse and worse, and there is a tidal wave of it. The insipid treacle we have the kids sing in school chapel is frequently nothing but a mud fence against that tidal wave.

Among conservative believers we at least have a concept of resistance to relativism in the areas of truth and ethics. We reject the idea that something can be true on Tuesday but false on Friday. We also reject the notion that sins in the first part of the week gradually lose their sinfulness by the weekend. But when it comes to aesthetics, we sound like a bunch of atheists in our defensive responses whenever someone tells us that the music we worship God with is the musical equivalent of a slab of Velveeta. As the Eagles so wonderfully exhorted us, we need to get over it.

We have to realize in this battle that we cannot fight something with nothing. This tidal wave of relativistic music (not to mention ninth-rate music) cannot be stopped by simply saying no. Nature abhors a vacuum, and children who are not taught to understand and appreciate good music will *not* spend the rest of their lives listening to no music. They will listen to lousy music. Obviously, the subject is an enormous one, but I am merely pointing out the road we need to take. What that road does after it disappears around the bend will be of great interest to us all then, but we cannot answer too many questions about it now.

Two basic issues should concern us as classical and Christian educators. First we have to be deeply concerned about our condoning musical illiteracy. We must not approach music literacy in a way that we would mock if anyone suggested it for verbal literacy—i.e., teaching music half an hour a week. In short, our goal should be to teach sight-reading of music to all our younger elementary students.

There is also the issue of familiarity with the canon of Western music. By this I do not mean "Git Along Little Doggies" music, but rather the music of Western culture. Throughout the course of their schooling, our students should be repeatedly exposed to the great musical tradition of Western civilization. In saying this, I am not excluding folk music, and I am certainly not excluding what might be called congregational music, most notably the psalms. Familiarity with the canon is not synonymous with elitist highbrow interests.

In this attempt, the school should honestly expect static. For any who doubted what was said above concerning relativism in the believing community, all their doubts will be swept away if they try to educate children's imagination in any of the ways laid out in this chapter. So do your homework and use your imagination.

19

CLASSICAL ATHLETICS

IN A WORLD THAT reels from one extreme to the next and then for good measure reels back again, balance is terribly hard to maintain. Nowhere is this difficulty more evident than in the vexing question of the relation of athletics to the classical Christian school.

Identifying the extremes is somewhat easy. But maintaining balance between them is where the practical problems arise. Even when the balance is temporarily obtained, pressure from outside makes it difficult to maintain. A man standing on the yellow line in the middle of the road looks as though he is perilously close to the left ditch—to the good folks living in the right ditch. And the people inhabiting the left ditch are very concerned about him too. Is he not *far* closer to the right ditch than they? Not only do they have these opinions, but they will usually act on them. A school administrator (or board) trying to sort these issues out in a balanced fashion will have to first answer this group and then that one. Sometimes the right decision means being thought out of balance by *everyone*.

On the question of athletics, the true extremes are worship of the body and contempt for the body. These views come quickly into play when a school board is deciding whether the school should field a football team or build a gymnasium or sponsor a girls' volleyball team. One contingent maintains that the school was established as a *school* and that the reason God gave boys and girls legs and feet was so that they could walk their brains to school. On the other side, equally extreme, are those who are dangerously close to sacrificing a heifer to the great god Football in their next halftime celebration. Given the quasi-religious fervor that grips many of these people, it is surprising that the Supreme Court has not yet struck down high school football programs as a clear violation of the so-called separation of church and state.

One of the first reactions of modern classical educators is to appeal to the prominent place of physical training and discipline in the ancient classical *paideia*. The obvious problem with this argument is the pagan assumptions that went into that training. The ancient classical emphasis was an idolatrous one. When Protagoras said that the measure of man was man, he was saying something that for the Hellenists had a clear physical component. Men were measured by their abilities in following a philosophical argument, but they were also measured by how far they could throw the discus. So although the tradition is an ancient one, Christian classical educators should not seek to justify their athletic programs by appealing to a bygone Olympiad.

The standard is always Scripture. We are not to build on ancient pagan foundations or on the fact that Dad was on the all-star football team when *he* was in high school. Nor is the foundation the overly intellectual tradition of the conservative Enlightenment that has contaminated a large portion of the modern Christian church. We must remember the ditches on both sides of the road.

We tend to think we must choose between subordinating the concerns of the mind to the body or, reversing this, subordinating the concerns of the body to the mind. In the former, we make sure the kids in the school get plenty of fresh air, exercise, dribbling skills practice, and so on. We try to work the academic schedule around this. In the latter, we ban recess in order to keep the kids at the grindstone of memorization. And it is easy to tell which way a school leans whenever the (inevitable) testing time comes.

That testing time is when the star player becomes academically ineligible. Will the school lower its academic expectations so that he can play Friday night? Or will pressure be put on the teachers to squeeze out a few extra points for this three-point shooter so that the team can squeeze out a few extra points? When this kind of situation develops, there will be two factions in the school. One wants to make academics serve the athletic program. The other wants to make the athletic program serve the curriculum, usually by eliminating it. Both are wrong.

There is no reason to give the brain priority over the body or vice versa. Both are to be submitted to the Scriptures. God tells the mind what to think, and He tells the body what to do. He always says what He says *to the whole person*. The issue is obedience to God, and not obedience of one part of a person to another part of that same person. Subordinating my bodily needs to my intellectual pursuits is as silly as asking whether my right foot should be in charge of my liver. They both should be subordinated to the Word of the Lord.

Someone may reply that the Bible teaches that the head has authority over the other parts of the body. But this statement is the victim of a metaphor. The head and the brain are as much a part of my body as anything else, and my hand is not "soul-less." I need oxygen to think as much as to run wind sprints. The body/brain dilemma in our schools, as it is popularly understood, is therefore a false one. At the same time, the Bible does teach a hierarchy of values. A man's spiritual/physical/emotional love for his wife is obviously more important than his toenail clippings. But everything that he is has spiritual and physical aspects, and these cannot be set off against one another. So we are to strive for a biblical balance.

Scripture teaches that bodily discipline is a good thing. Paul was very comfortable with using athletic imagery. For example, he compared the Christian life to a foot race, which would be an odd thing to do if athletic competition were somehow inherently sinful.

Know ye not that they which run in a race run all, but one receiveth the prize? So run, that ye may obtain. And every man that striveth for the mastery is temperate in all things. Now they do it to obtain a corruptible crown; but we an incorruptible. I therefore so run, not as uncertainly; so fight I, not as one that beateth the air: But I keep under my body, and bring it into subjection: lest that by any means, when I have preached to others, I myself should be a castaway. (1 Cor. 9:24-27)

In another place Paul says that he is pressing toward the *prize*—the trophy. "Brethren, I count not myself to have apprehended: but this one thing I do, forgetting those things which are behind, and reaching forth unto those things which are before, I press toward the mark for the prize of the high calling of God in Christ Jesus" (Phil. 3:13-14). He established our priorities for us in this regard: "For bodily exercise profiteth little: but godliness is profitable unto all things, having promise of the life that now is, and of that which is to come" (1 Tim. 4:8).

If we are to live by every word that proceeds from the mouth of God, and if godliness is profitable in all things, then godliness is profitable in the realm of athletics. In other words, if the athletic program is not helping the kids understand God, man, sin, and salvation, then the program is failing, regardless of the win/loss record. But the same thing is true of the "classroom program."

The point of everything is discipleship. The point of everything we do is the high calling of following Christ. So every athletic program should be measured in exactly the same way as the classroom instruction. The question for everyone should be this: "How does your program specifically reflect the authority of the Lord Jesus Christ, and in what ways is the program distinctively Christian?" If the football coach cannot answer the question, then it does not matter if he is the "winningest ever." And there is no double standard. The same question goes to the English teacher and the band instructor.

I am familiar with classical Christian schools that have fallen into both excesses. But my use of the word *excess* here refers to their emphasis being out of balance with the teaching of Scripture, not out of balance with some false mind/body competition. Some minimize recess or P.E. in order to maximize that all-important "brain time." Some try to turn physical education into an academic pursuit, instead of what it ought to be—pursuit of the ball. Other schools show every indication of pursuing the same athletic idols worshiped in all the area government schools. An example of this kind of folly would be a school that accepts state accreditation in order to make it possible for their kids to compete in district or state competitions. Thus they have accepted unbelieving control of their curriculum in exchange for a chance to compete against secular schools athletically. In other words, they have ceased to "compete" with the government schools across the board so that they can compete with them in a very narrow area, usually for just a few days a year.

When a school says, "An athletic program is not necessarily inconsistent with Christianity," the response should be that this is quite right. But it *can* be inconsistent even if it need not be. So the question must be asked: "In what ways specifically is the program different from one that *is* inconsistent with a Christian worldview?" For those who would solve the problem by banning athletic programs, the question is similar: "In what ways is your total opposition to an athletic program distinctively Christian?"

We would soon discover that many of our opinions on both sides are not grounded in Scripture. If we would have a consistent Christian academy, we have to be able to answer questions about all that we do. One obvious place to begin concerns the different requirements the Bible places on boys and girls.

By having an athletic program or P.E. classes with a Christian goal or direction, we answer questions about the threat of gnosticism. By having rigorous academic standards that are not sacrificed to the idol of a sports program, we answer the objection that a school's priorities are misplaced. We stand with Luther, who considered "gymnastics" of value both for the body and the soul.[1]

LIFE IN THE CHRISTIAN SCHOOL

20

PERSONAL HOLINESS

EVERY SIGNIFICANT PROBLEM a classical school will ever face will be related in some way to unconfessed sin. Put another way, the school has only one enemy, one problem to conquer, and that is the problem of sin.

Now confession of sin and personal holiness do not refer to the same thing. Confession of sin is a *sine qua non* of personal holiness, but it is not the same thing as personal holiness. Growth in grace is not the immediate result of a negative process. If a houseplant is knocked over, and the pot is broken, the plant must be repotted if it is to continue to grow. But repotting a plant is not the same thing as the plant growing. Without the replanting the growth will not happen, but the replanting does not automatically ensure growth.

Growth in grace depends on the means of grace established by God: Word and sacrament, faithful worship, practical obedience. But if unconfessed sin is deliberately ignored, the growth will always be stunted, no matter how much the means of grace are applied. The shattered pot and houseplant on the floor can be faithfully watered and the curtains pulled back so that sunlight gets to it, but the plant is still doomed. Far too many Christians attend worship services, sing hymns and psalms, and partake of the Lord's Supper, but they still cling to their sins, refusing to confess them. They forget that all their behavior is before the presence of the God who has said that He cannot endure iniquity and solemn assembly (Isa. 1:13).

Confession of sin, keeping short accounts, is therefore essential to the spiritual health of a school community. After all, for an average-size school, three hundred sinners spend five days a week together there, for eight hours a day for nine months. If such a school had no janitor, just imagine what the bathrooms would look like after three days. What about the halls? In the same way, because the importance of confession of sin is neglected, many schools operate without any spiritual janitor. Everybody makes a mess, but nobody picks up. When this condition becomes part of the culture of the school, with niggling sins left lying about, a day of reckoning comes when the place blows up—the headmaster runs off with the secretary, and everyone is flummoxed. "How could this happen? This is a *Christian* school."

But long ago David showed the progression of sin: "Who can understand his errors? Cleanse thou me from secret faults. Keep back thy servant also from presumptuous sins; let them not have dominion over me: then shall I be upright, and I shall be innocent from the great transgression" (Ps. 19:12-13).

David asked for cleansing from *secret* sin. He asked also that God would deliver him from *presumptuous* sins. Then he said that he would be kept back from the *great* transgression. The headmaster in my example tolerated secret sin. He, and others in the school, tolerated sins of presumption—displays of temper, manifestations of self-centeredness, and so on. When such sins reach a certain level, there are no resources to fight off the temptation to those great sins that wreck lives, families, schools, and communities. Yet everyone assumed that the headmaster was a godly man, walking in the light, until three days before the adultery.

So what is true confession? A person who confesses sin is doing something like this: In prayer to God, he names the sin, taking care to use the same name that the Bible uses. He does this because he is repentant and has turned away from that sin, rejecting it entirely. He thanks God for His promised forgiveness and resolves by God's grace to make restitution where appropriate. Such restitution is necessary with sins such as lying, theft, open bitterness, and sexual infidelity.

Scripture is very clear on the need for confession: "He that covereth his sins shall not prosper: but whoso confesseth and forsaketh them shall have mercy" (Prov. 28:13). And the Word is equally clear that He will surely forgive: "If we confess our sins, he is faithful and just to forgive us our sins, and to cleanse us from all unrighteousness" (1 John 1:9).

We have to be careful in dealing with this area. We must first consider what confession of sin is and is not. Unless we think properly about this, we will stumble doctrinally, and instead of receiving help from our confession, we will get ourselves into a horrible mess. One of the first principles to remember is that confession is not meritorious—to confess sins as a way of placing God in one's debt is not dealing with sin; it is committing *another* sin. The context of all confession must be a thorough grasp of the free grace of justification. Put another way, confession is one of the duties of our sanctification; it is not something we contribute to our justification.

Positively stated, confession is agreement. The word for *confess* in 1 John 1:9 is *homologeo*, which means that we are to agree with God about our sin. It means "to speak the same." Adultery is adultery and not "an inappropriate relationship." Lying is lying and not "creative diplomacy."

We also have to make sure our motives for confession are right. There are many good motives, but three motives for confession should be sufficient to encourage us to do what we need to do. First, confession is required by God; God requires believers to confess their sins in an ongoing way. The texts we have considered make the point very plain. To obey Him in any way glorifies Him, and obedience in this matter is no exception. Obedience is a sufficient motive. Second, confession of sin protects loved ones; in the context we have been discussing, it protects the school. Because Achan hid his sin, the nation of Israel was defeated in battle, and his family was executed. We never sin in isolation, however hidden we may believe the sin to be. And third, confession restores the soul. God disciplines us when we are living with unconfessed sin, a truth we see plainly in Scripture. "For whom the Lord loveth he chasteneth, and scourgeth every son whom he receiveth" (Heb. 12:6). God dealt severely with David in his sin. "For day and night thy hand was heavy upon me" (Ps. 32:4). Because this is disciplinary and not punitive, the sooner we learn the lesson and confess, the better it is for us. Moreover, confession establishes the soul. The difference between an unrepentant sinner and believers who are walking with God is *not* that he or she sins and they do not. The difference is found in the fact that they pick up after themselves.

But we still run from God's chastening. We do not want the blow to our pride that confession of sin brings. Confession is clearly the right thing to do but still hard to swallow. So we come up with many reasons for not swallowing.

One of the things we do is *trivialize the sin:* We say that it is too small to confess. We do not want to annoy God with our petty problems. A teacher takes some equipment that was set aside for another teacher and hides it away. "It is too petty to bring up now." Or perhaps we *surrender to the sin:* We say that the sin is too big to confess; it is more powerful than God, and we give up all attempts to be free of it. This is the counsel of despair (Isa. 1:18). Perhaps the sin is something like the use of a school computer to download porn. "I can't confess *that!* I'd get fired."

We may *justify the sin*, saying that what we did was really all right. The adulteress wipes her mouth and says she has done no wrong (Prov. 30:20). "I know I called Billy's mother that name, but she deserved it. About time someone stood up to her." And we *excuse the sin*, admitting that our behavior was wrong, but claiming extenuating circumstances. Saul excused his sin when Samuel did not arrive on time, and the soldiers were deserting the army (1 Sam. 13:12). "I know I shouldn't have said that to Billy's mother, but she started it." Another tactic is to *blur the sin:* We do this through the use of vague terms. We want forgiveness for "anything we might have done." "God, the bad attitudes at the school are getting out of hand." Whose bad attitudes? When?

Another popular approach is to *reassign the sin:* We blame someone else. Consider the example of Adam and Eve: "The *woman* You gave me." "The *serpent* beguiled me." A headmaster may refuse to take responsibility for what happens in the school and simply blame the staff.

We can *ignore the sin:* We hope that the problem will disappear if we ignore it long enough. We hope that everything will just fix itself. We look the other way. A similar technique is *putting off dealing with the sin:* We know that the sin will have to be dealt with sometime and so, we reason, why not tomorrow? But the Bible says that if we hear His voice *today*, we should not harden our hearts (Heb. 4:7). "I know I have to seek their forgiveness sometime. Maybe later." Another method is to *hide the sin:* Adam and Eve sought to do this in the Garden (Gen. 3:8). They heard the Maker of heaven and earth coming, so they decided to hide in the bushes. "Nobody knows about this, and nobody needs to know about it. I asked Sally to keep my indiscreet comments between the two of us."

The method employed by the very proud is to *embrace the sin:* This is rebellion and defiance. We say that we will not confess—a common response when the sin is anger, bitterness, or pride. "This school is filled with hypocrites anyway. I don't owe *them* anything." Or we could *buy the sin:* This happens when restitution is required, and we see the cost as too high to pay. But of course, true restitution is not a cost at all. "I know I shouldn't have taken those books home, but I can't tell anybody now. What would they say? I might lose my job."

And last there are those who *theologize the sin:* We do this when we have important doctrinal or theological reasons for our refusal to confess. "I am justified, so I don't need to." "The corporate confession at church is adequate" (1 John 1:10). "I am the Bible teacher. I know that what I did was wrong, but I was teaching the kids just yesterday that Christ forgives all our sins, past, present, and future. It's all under the blood."

But it is impossible to make a good omelet with rotten eggs. If staff members of a Christian school are not walking in fellowship with God, then they cannot be in fellowship with one another. If we walk in the light, John says, we have fellowship with one another (1 John 1:7). If the people working in the school are under the chastening hand of God, then it does not matter how many education conferences they go to. It does not matter how intelligent they are. It does not matter how many books they read. It does not matter that they have adopted a classical Christian curriculum. The whole thing stinks. The enterprise is comparable to insisting on rotten eggs as ingredients and then determining to make the omelet good by improving the kitchen, firing the cook, or changing the recipe. Refusal to deal with sin as sin is folly, pure and simple.

The second aspect of personal holiness in the school has to do with the rejection of all such folly and the pursuit of wisdom. A society is known by its proverbs—what it values and what it does not, where it professes to find wisdom and where it does not. Our modern culture hates objectivity; countless propaganda pieces tell us that we must find the truth within ourselves, we must be true to ourselves, we must always believe in ourselves, *ad nauseam*. But the Word of God says, "He that trusteth in his own heart *is a fool*: but whoso walketh wisely, he shall be delivered" (Prov. 28:26). But shouldn't we express ourselves? "A *fool* gives full vent to his spirit, but a wise man quietly holds it back" (Prov. 29:11 ESV; *cf.* 18:2).

And because we are rightly concerned that a wise man will see right through this stupidity of ours, we disparage and demean the importance of moral knowledge. Tragically, Christians have led the way *in this folly*. But, "The heart of the prudent getteth *knowledge*; and the ear of the wise seeketh *knowledge*" (Prov. 18:15; *cf.* 24:5).

Wisdom and folly are moral issues. Proverbs teaches clearly that the fear of the Lord is the very start of wisdom (Prov. 1:7; 9:10). Wisdom is clearly the gift of a gracious God. "For the LORD gives wisdom; from His mouth come knowledge and understanding; he stores up sound wisdom for the upright; he is a shield to those who walk in integrity" (Prov. 2:6-7 ESV). Wisdom and folly bring two inevitable results: "The wise shall inherit *glory:* but *shame* shall be the promotion of fools" (Prov. 3:35).

Further, wisdom is important: "Wisdom is *the principal thing*; therefore get wisdom: and with all thy getting get understanding" (Prov. 4:7). In all our getting—scholarships, promotions, increased enrollments, awards, etc.—make sure that the one thing needful is not missing. *Get wisdom.*

Teachers must be themselves teachable. One of the clearest distinctions in Proverbs between the wise man and fool is their respective attitudes toward rebuke, correction, or instruction. A fool needs it desperately and will not have it. A wise man needs it far less and welcomes it gladly. "A wise man will hear and increase learning; and a man of understanding shall attain unto wise counsels" (Prov. 1:5; *cf.* 10:8). A word will do for a wise man what a club won't do for a fool. "A rebuke goes deeper into a man of understanding than a hundred blows into a fool" (Prov. 17:10 ESV). There's no real sense in talking to a fool. "Do not speak in the hearing of a fool, for he will despise the good sense of your words" (Prov. 23:9 ESV).

The wise are diligent. Wisdom is a moral attribute; it is not surprising to find wisdom connected to things such as work, just as folly is to laziness. "Go to the ant, O sluggard; consider her ways, and *be wise*" (Prov. 6:6 ESV). Wise men are producers; fools have their identity as *consumers.* ". . . a foolish man spendeth it up" (Prov. 21:20).

The fool is self-important: "The way of a fool is *right in his own eyes*, but a wise man listens to advice" (Prov. 12:15 ESV). The wise man is humble: "One who is wise is cautious and turns away from evil, but a fool is reckless and careless" (Prov. 14:16 ESV). The saying is that beauty is only skin deep, but ugly goes clean to the bone. Scripture gives us an application to folly: "Crush a fool in a mortar with a pestle along with crushed grain, yet his folly will not depart from him" (Prov. 27:22 ESV).

In our egalitarian times, we never want folly to be publicly labeled as such. But the Bible does not mince words. The fool should be recognized. The Bible teaches that it is not *seemly* for a fool to be honored. "As snow in summer, and as rain in harvest, so honour is not seemly for a fool" (Prov. 26:1). In addition, it is not even seemly for a fool to pretend to be something else. "Excellent speech becometh not a fool" (Prov. 17:7). This includes excellent speeches at education conferences and lectures in classrooms. If for no other reason, fools should be identified simply out of self-defense. Because they do not have yellow warning stickers attached to their foreheads, we must use the biblical criteria. As we stay away from fools, we must also seek out the wise: "Whoever walks with the wise becomes wise, but the companion of fools will suffer harm" (Prov. 13:20 ESV).

The application to our schools should be plain. If we humbly receive the duty God places on us, the duty of confession of sin, we are walking the path of wisdom. If we refuse it, then we have embraced folly. Now every Christian school has a culture of its own. The fundamental question every educator reading this should ask is this: Does our school have a culture of ready, humble confession? Or does it have the only alternative—a culture of defensiveness, posturing, deceit, and bitterness? And which school will be blessed by God?

21

BOARDSMANSHIP

MORE OFTEN THAN NOT, Christian schools are run by school boards. Not surprisingly, if the board is wise, the school is blessed. If the board is foolish, the school suffers. Sometimes the school is lucky.

The period of luck is usually the early years. The founders are dedicated and would crawl over broken glass to get the school up and running. Everyone is running on a good deal of adrenaline, coffee, prayer, and high hopes. Everybody does everything wrong, and nobody cares, because the adrenaline rush of starting a school covers a multitude of sins. But after a time, the school is finally established, a headmaster is hired, policies are in place, and the board looks around, only to discover that they are still meeting once a week, and they are still debating the toilet paper rotation procedures.

This is the time when certain "board sins" start catching up with a school. In the front rank of such sins is confusion about the nature of corporate authority. One of the most common problems in board-run schools is the assumption made by strong-willed board members (a redundancy, I know) that they constitute in their own person the full authority of the board. But this is not the case. A basic necessity here is that boards must understand what constitutes board action and what does not.

Here is a common scenario. A board member has an idea going, and he wants to present this idea at the next board meeting. But he needs some information, and so he goes to the bookkeeper or to the third grade teacher and asks her to collect information for his report. If asked what authority he has to do this, he would respond with a quizzical look. He's a *board* member. But the authority of a board is corporate, and each individual board member as an individual has no authority whatever. The board vests authority in the individuals to act in a particular capacity and no further. The board does not have the authority that the individuals bring to it, but rather the other way around. The only time an individual board member has this kind of authority is when the collective board explicitly gives it to him.

Board authority is *collective*. Consequently, every Christian school board needs to understand that board action has only occurred if a motion is made at a duly constituted board meeting, is seconded, is carried by the appropriate number of votes, the results recorded in the minutes, and the minutes subsequently approved. Then at that point we can say that the board has acted. If an individual board member goes off on his own, he is doing so without any board authority at all. He is just another parent. A reasonable request that would be granted to any parent should of course be granted to him, but does he represent the board? Not unless the board has said so.

Although it should not have to be said, all this goes double for board members' wives. At the same time, teachers or administrators can easily be intimidated into thinking that they had better do what a board member asks, whether or not there was any board action. Once these assumptions take root in the school, it is just a matter of time before the disaster.

A related issue is the question of disagreements that arise on the board. If the disagreement is one of fundamental principle, and the vote goes against the principled board member, it is appropriate to voice disagreement publicly, but only because the issue is important enough to fight over to the last ditch—say, the proposed hiring of a homosexual chorus director. But if the disagreement is more routine, e.g., do we use this Christian textbook or that one, then once the vote is taken, each board member is called to accept the action of the whole board. Even if the vote was divided, the vote determined what the whole board would do. In the case of split votes, individual board members who dissent should take a page from Trumpkin the dwarf:

> "But I thought you didn't believe in the Horn, Trumpkin," said Caspian. "No more I do, your Majesty. But what's that got to do with it? I might as well die on a wild goose chase as die here. You are my King. I know the difference between giving advice and taking orders. You've had my advice, and it's the time for orders."[1]

This attitude is difficult to achieve in real situations, but it is most necessary. The application here is really nothing less than a covenantal humility of mind. I gave an illustration of this in *Repairing the Ruins:*

> Suppose further that you are now at the meeting where the new text-books are being announced, the minority board member is chairing the meeting, and a parent in the back row objects. He lists seven compelling reasons why the other textbooks should have been selected. They are the same seven compelling reasons that the chairmen himself presented last week at the board meeting. Now the chairman only has a biblical view of authority if he now stands publicly with the rest of the board.... "We thought we should choose these textbooks because . . ."[2]

It is also crucial for board members to recognize the importance of basic worldview agreement. Amos asks if two can walk together if they are not in agreement. How much less is it possible for a board of seven people to get anything done if they are profoundly divided among themselves? Of course, board members will differ about many issues that come before them—that is part of the point of having a board. A board takes advantage of the different perspectives on this budget item or that one, whether this teacher should be hired or that one, and so on. But we must beware of pluralistic assumptions creeping into our views of how a board should be constituted. We have gotten to the point that we think of diversity as automatically a good thing. The Scriptures require like-mindedness of Christians (Rom. 15:5), and this requirement is not set aside in the case of school boards. You should strive for as much like-mindedness as you can get. At a bare minimum all the board members should embrace the school's statement of faith robustly. In a similar way, the board members must be of one mind on what constitutes a classical and Christian education. If they are not, then the only possible result is an attempt, at some level, to pull the school in different directions.

The board must be diligent to guard against "mission drift." One of the first things we notice in this world is the presence of entropy. Left unattended, things fall apart. Poorly attended, things fall apart. A garden left to its own devices will soon be full of weeds. When a school is finally established, it has a good deal of "sweat equity" invested in it. Given that and given the fact of entropy, it is astonishing how quickly many people forget to watch over what they have built.

Further, entropy simply points to a natural process in a fallen world. But the things happening to the school are not just the result of natural processes (although some of them are). Remember that we are engaged in a spiritual war, and there is another army out there doing its level best to accelerate entropy in your midst. In other words, the school will be attacked. Vigilance is important at all times, but in a time of war, it is prudent to post sentries. One of the basic tasks of the board is to be that sentry. Is the school staying true to its founding vision?

A failure here is mission drift. Fortunately, there are danger signs; there are certain things your sentries can watch for. The first is economic pragmatism. Making the school "work" is not pragmatism but simply competence. However, discussions of making "it" work without concern for the content of "it" are examples of pragmatism. What is regularly at the top of the board agenda? Curriculum discussion or schemes for attracting donors?

Another problem is democracy. When individuals associated with the school want to affect the direction and vision of the school simply because they are *there*, the school is in danger. Parents who have had their children enrolled for five years *should* have an understanding of the school's vision (and it is the task of the school to communicate that vision), but many times such parents want their time at the school to serve as their qualification to suggest that everything the school stands for should be scratched: "Why don't we drop Latin? My Johnny doesn't like it."

A board should be eager to support godly discipline in the school by backing up the administrators. Lack of discipline will kill your school— a school without discipline has no way to fight off "infections." If a school is unwilling or unable to fire administrators or teachers, expel or suspend students, *the school will take on the mission desired by those the school refuses to let go.* The troublemakers can determine, rightly, that the board wants to do it the troublemakers' way instead of the way set out in the founding vision of the school.

A board must not develop a fear of ideas. When a board becomes leery of pedagogical debate, the end is in sight. They are the board of a *school*. Is the board of GM upset when their engineers try to improve the design of their cars? Theological apathy is another problem. It has been said earlier that a person who does not stand for something will fall for anything. The school must have theological definition beyond a mere evangelical vanilla-ism. There are some appalling theologies floating around in the world of modern evangelicalism, and if the school says it mattereth not, then that school deserves everything it gets, good and hard. And, of course, another related danger is that posed by the forces of political correctness. If the board members find themselves doing things that they do not want to do, for fear of the bad press they will get, then the school is toast.

To conclude the chapter, an outline of basic board duties should be helpful. With all this in mind, whither and what? These are the basic board duties:[3]

The board is responsible for *appreciation, recognition, and encouragement*—particularly with the headmaster or superintendent, who answers directly to the board. He, in turn, is responsible to give the same to his staff. One of the great failings of boards is to be constantly critical. Every board should take steps to make sure that this first duty is fulfilled.

The board is responsible for *decision-making*. The buck stops at the board. The decisions it makes should be contained for the most part in the school's policy manual. A board that makes every decision *ad hoc* is likely a micro-managing body. An administrator should have most of the board's decisions in a notebook on his desk. He should be able to seek the board's wisdom for most situations without talking to the board. If a truly unique situation comes up, he can take it to the board. And if that unique situation looks like it might happen again, the board should give the administrator a policy on it. A board that just wings it can make lots of decisions, but at the end of the day, the administrator will be stuck with a Talmud-like conglomeration of precedents, *ad hoc* decisions, and half-remembered conversations.

The board is also responsible for the *master plan*. Where is the school going to build? How big will it get? These are not policy decisions of the day-to-day variety. Rather, they have to do with the larger vision of what the school will become in the community. The board is responsible for this plan.

The board members should be people of influence in a community, and they should be able to bring resources to bear in a way that will help the school. The board should be good at *networking*.

The board *maintains an overview* of the school. Because the board members do not spend all day, every day at the school, they have the advantage of distance (as well as, of course, the disadvantage of distance). But when a board knows its business, it can evaluate a school fairly from that vantage point.

The board is responsible for *problem-solving*. One of the more common problems would be a budget shortfall in the spring. The board approves the budget, and if the superintendent has mismanaged it, that should of course show up in the superintendent's evaluation. But in the meantime, the creditors want their money. The board is responsible to take leadership in times of crisis. In such cases the board has to be careful not to undercut the administration, but the responsibility for problem-solving at a certain level is the board's.

The board is responsible for two kinds of *record keeping*. A means of determining whether all necessary records are being kept—financial, health, grades, etc.—should be part of the board's regular evaluation of the school and the administration. And, of course, secondly, the board is responsible to keep its own minutes.

The board is responsible to *hire, evaluate, and fire, if necessary, the senior administrator* of the school. The board should not try to reach past him to control anything in the school. They have authority over the school, but they exercise it through him, not in spite of him. They should give him clear and useful direction and evaluate how he did in following out those directives. If he has done poorly, he serves at the pleasure of the board.

The board is responsible to set the tone for *spiritual leadership*. Every board member should meet the basic moral qualifications for leadership set down in Scripture for elders, with due allowances made for differences in calling. Board members do not have to be gifted teachers, for example. But all board members should be practicing, confessing Christians, men who take their faith with them wherever they go and with a serious joy. Their faith should be evident to everyone, particularly those associated with the school who have dealings with the board.

In all these things, the board is responsible to *maintain an expectation of excellence*. If the board does not maintain high standards for the classical Christian school, it is unlikely that anyone else will do it.

SCHOOL CLOTHES

SCHOOLS THAT ARE just starting should save themselves a lot of trouble by establishing a clear definition of appropriate school clothing at the very beginning. The standard should either be a school uniform or clearly established guidelines for what is considered appropriate. Such a policy enables the administration to set the tone for the school positively rather than negatively.

If a school simply has a dress code that says the students, for example, are not to be immodest, they will soon discover how many different ways there are to be immodest and how many differing understandings of modesty there are within the Christian community. Simply saying, "Wear this," solves a lot of these practical problems. The value of maintaining high standards can be clearly seen in the hallways and classrooms of the school, while at the same time the administrators and teachers do not have to spend a good deal of their time as fashion police. Rather they can concentrate on teaching. Of course, if a school adopts a strict dress code because they *like* wasting their time, they can obsess about whether a girl's barrettes match her uniform's socks.

If an established school has had virtually no dress code or a negatively defined code, and that school tries to come around to school uniforms or clothes, there will likely be a controversy. Moreover, many of the objections will come from the parents and not the students. What might be called the "casual imperative" has established itself in the American mind as the ultimate *desideratum*. Whatever else you do in the morning when you dress, make sure you make yourself comfortable.

Of course, we *should* dress for comfort, but the biblical view is that we should also dress for the comfort of *others*. Today our natural tendency is to dress to suit *ourselves*. In another era, students would dress to make themselves presentable. Now students want to dress to make themselves at ease. The former generations thought of others; we now insist on putting ourselves first.

A school is a community of students and scholars, and the dress should be suitable for the task at hand, part of which is living with one another in an academic setting. School clothes should be "dress that is designated as appropriate to a student's vocational calling."[1] A school should be a place where the students are being taught to live incarnationally, with the things they are being taught coming out their fingertips, translating into their words, actions, gestures, and clothing. As I wrote elsewhere:

> In all this, we must remember the centrality of peripherals. The point is not to favor the peripherals *instead* of the center. That would be the sin of majoring on minors, swallowing camels, and all the rest of it. Rather, the point is that on this question the Christian world has fallen into the fallacy of bifurcation. Either we emphasize the center and wave off the peripherals as unimportant, or we emphasize the peripherals and forget the center. But remember, the fruit—which Christ required for identifying the nature of a tree—is way out on the edges of the tree and at the farthest point away from the root. We must recover the notion that peripherals are central because the center is important.[2]

The Enlightenment tradition insists on the primacy of "timeless truths" and says that as long as a student gets the answer right, nailing down that timeless truth, it does not matter if the answer came out of a disheveled, greasy head. It does not matter if the student mumbling the timeless truth is slouching around the place. Externals do not matter—only the Euclidian proof in the head. In contrast to this, the Christian approach is incarnational and insists on discipling the whole person. Everything is to brought into submission to the Lord Jesus Christ, and every thought is to be made captive, every collar obedient, and every pair of slacks honoring to Him (2 Cor. 10:4-5).

So what does the Bible actually teach about clothing? Modern evangelicals like to assume that their lives accord with Scripture, and so they often assert that Scripture says nothing about what kind of clothes we are to wear. But this idea is suspended on nothing but people's own desires. The Bible says a great deal about clothing.

We have already considered how relativism has poured into the church in the realm of aesthetics. Believing Christians maintain the faith when it comes to truth. We know that if Jesus is Lord on Monday, then He is also Lord on Friday. We have kept the faith also when it comes to basic ethical issues. Moral relativism is rejected; if stealing and abortion are wrong at all, they are wrong in every generation. The passage of time does not alter the authority of God's Ten Commandments. But the triad we want to urge in classical Christian education is truth, goodness, and *beauty*. When it comes to aesthetic issues, the Christian world is horribly compromised. One of the tasks of the Christian school is to help bring us out of this aesthetic relativism by teaching students to love that which is lovely—in music, in painting, in poetry, in drama, and in dress. Whatever is *lovely*, Paul says, think on this.

When the Bible says that Abigail was a beautiful and intelligent woman (1 Sam. 25:3), this means that there is such a thing as feminine loveliness. When the Bible calls us to sing a new song to God and to play skillfully with a shout of joy (Ps. 33:1), this means that there is such a thing as a skillful performance in music. Such references (and there are many) are in themselves sufficient to show that aesthetic relativism is contrary to the Scriptures. But our specific subject is clothes, and more specifically clothes in a school setting.

The Bible tells us that some clothes are nicer than others. Rebekah took Esau's *choice clothes* and put them on her son Jacob (Gen. 27:15). God rebuked the city of Tyre, a merchant city that trafficked in *choice items*, among which were purple clothes and embroidered garments (Ezek. 27:24). Achan was tempted by a beautiful Babylonian garment and not by a pair of sweats (Josh. 7:21). Ruth presented herself to Boaz in her best garments (Ruth 3:3). Such passages simply state what everyone in the world knows (as long as no debate over school clothes is in process): Some clothes are better than others.

But the next issue is also important for a school to recognize. Some clothes are more *suitable* than others. Clothes are tailored for the occasion. There is no reason for a man to rent a tux in order to change the oil in his car. A tux is a better garment than a mechanic's overalls, in the abstract, but when we consider the task at hand, we may much prefer the overalls. So we should recognize that while a girl's formal dress is nicer than her school uniform, her school uniform is more suitable for math class. The Scriptures recognize this vocational aspect of clothing as well. John the Baptist had the calling of a desert prophet, and he dressed accordingly (Matt. 11:8). He did not wear the soft clothing of first-century politicians. Jesus altered His dress in order to wash the disciples' feet (John 13:4, 12). Simon Peter took off his outer garment in order to fish (John 21:7).

Now some might point out that James tells us not to make judgments about people based on their external appearance, and this is quite true (James 2:2-3). Moreover we should teach our students not to make such superficial judgments, and this is another compelling reason why the school should require a defined form of suitable school dress. Left to themselves, the students will establish their own informal dress code. This is another inescapable concept: It is not *whether* there will be cultural enforcement of dress standards, but *which* standards will be applied and by whom.

When a school does not exercise leadership in student dress, the students do not leave one another alone. What happens is that the "cool kids" establish a pattern of dress, and woe betide a nerdy kid who does not conform. He is not sent home to change by the principal; he is simply shunned by the other kids. In short, the kind of malicious and wicked judgments that James forbids take root in the school. But if a school exercises wise leadership here, the students can be taught to love one another in the way they dress. There *will* be a dress code—whether the students establish it based on whims and fads or the school establishes it based on careful biblical reflection. If the students establish it, conformity will still be required, but in a stealthy kind of way. That uniform will probably involve torn denim. But Alfred E. Newman put it well sometime in the sixties: "Today's nonconformists are getting harder and harder to tell apart."

This discipline in clothing would be appropriate even if we were not living in the midst of general cultural disintegration. The school uniform in a stable society would simply distinguish the students of the classical Christian academy from the students in the Roman Catholic school across town, in the same way that Fed Ex drivers differ from UPS drivers. But we do live in the midst of a cultural meltdown, and so I should conclude with a few comments about that.

A few years ago I was talking to a woman about what has happened to our standards of dress. She told me a story that illustrated the point quite well. When she was a student at the University of Idaho, one Christmas break she thought she could go up to the administration building to pick up her grades. But despite the fact that it was a break, she ran into the dean of women, who cited her for being on the campus without wearing a dress. This was in 1965. In short, in 1965 a secular university had higher standards for dress than most Christian schools have today. For those who remember what happened to our culture in the late sixties, the situation was changed by something other than a simple shift in fashion tastes. We are talking here about something far more important than wide ties or narrow ties.

Young people today are desperately trying to vandalize the image of God that they carry about, despite themselves, in their bodies. God gave long hair to women as a glory and a covering—showing that the Lord is near—and yet bewildered, unprotected, and lost women now cut their hair with hedge clippers and dye it bizarre colors. An ancient statement reapplied is *apropos*. Augustine, quoting Cyprian, said, "Staining your hair is a piece of reckless audacity and blasphemous contempt; experimenting with orange tints in your hair is an omen of hell-fire."[3] The current practice of tattooing and mutilating the body resembles the self-loathing of the priests of Baal more than anything that should be seen among Christians. The wearing of clothing that does not fit, does not flatter, and does not proclaim the lordship of Christ is commonplace, and unbelievers will frankly acknowledge that this is the statement they are *trying* to make through their appearance. They are trying to proclaim the autonomy of self, and while they are at it, they are declaring how miserable such autonomous selves are.

But modern evangelical Christians, who have an eagle eye when it comes to imitating anything the world does, are blind to *why* the world is doing it. Unfortunate souls are trying to develop a cultural form of dress that says, "I am lost and hopelessly damned." And we have Christians who seriously want to imitate this or allow it into the hallways of Christian schools, saying all the while that we can make it mean something like, "Christians are on the cutting edge too." But actually it just shows that we are terminally clueless. Imitators of the world's culture from within the church know everything about the world's culture— *except what it means.*

This desire to fit in or to be thought cool is not a new phenomenon. The Bible calls it worldliness (1 John 2:12-17). All this is bad enough as a phenomenon within the broader Christian world. But for the board, administrators, and teachers of a Christian school, to be culturally clueless is disaster.

23

THE SEVEN LAWS OF
TEACHING

THE SEVEN LAWS OF TEACHING has been used at Logos School in
our teacher training for many years. Written in the nineteenth century
by John Milton Gregory, the principles or laws that he outlines are in fact
principles and are not focused, as so much modern teacher training is, on
mere methods. Methods are important enough in their place, but principles must be mastered *first*.[1] The point of this chapter is simply to state
each of the laws, summarize the application of them, and encourage the
reader to pursue the study of Gregory's work. Every classical Christian
school ought to have this work as an essential part of its teacher training,
and every teacher, veteran or novice, should be able to apply each of the
laws to what is done in the classroom.

The first law is this: "A teacher must be one who knows the lesson
or truth or art to be taught."

In the first place, the necessity of this law might seem self-evident.
How can water flow uphill, or how can a ball of darkness shed light?
But many teachers have drifted into practices that contradict this principle when they act more like a study hall monitor or proctor, assuming that the book has the material, and they can just check the student's
performance against the teacher's edition of the book. This is not
teaching.

Much of our modern teaching industry is dedicated to a neglect of
this law. Teachers get degrees in education, which is a far cry from a
teacher of history getting a degree in history. The tendency of modern
education departments is to emphasize the methods of teaching rather
than the content of what is to be taught. A case could be made for

instruction in such methods, but the person being instructed should already have training in the substance of what he or she will teach.

Some important things flow from the recognition of this law. Gregory sees the importance of illustration in teaching and notes how mastery of the material is the only basis for apt illustration.[2] If teachers do not have the material at their fingertips, they cannot draw from it in order to illustrate different aspects of the lesson. The only thing they can teach is what is on the page of the textbook.

Enthusiasm is also related to good teaching, and the apathetic refusal to learn the material cannot translate into enthusiasm in teaching it. As Gregory puts it, the "final product of clear thought is clear speech."[3]

The second law is that a "learner is one who attends with interest to the lesson." The ideal situation here for the learner is when two conditions pertain. The student is disciplined and gives active attention to the lesson. The material is fascinating in its own right and compels attention readily.

Education is not mere "data transfer." We are not moving around ones and zeros. The student must *think*. In Gregory's words, "Ideas can be communicated only by inducing in the receiving mind processes corresponding to those by which these ideas were first conceived."[4] The receiving mind is not a bucket into which the teacher drops things.

While the student has obvious duties in this process, the teacher is the one responsible to see that the student's duties are being accomplished. Teachers must know they have the attention of the students. They should alter their behavior as signs of student fatigue set in. They should have thought-provoking questions established *beforehand*. Attentiveness on the part of the students cannot be compelled across the board. And if teachers are bored by this material, they are teaching the students to have the same attitude.

The third law is that the "language used as a medium between teacher and learner must be common to both."

The teacher must *stoop* in order to teach. She has to step into the language known by the student in order to expand the power and extent of that language. In Gregory's words, "the teacher must come within this sphere of the child's language power if he would be understood."[5] Nothing is accomplished if big words whistle over the children's heads. The point is to teach in such a way that the students grow into new territory. But the teacher must stand in territory common to both teacher and student in order to do this. The power of illustration comes into play again here. Gregory notes the effectiveness of the parables of Jesus, drawn from *the known world* of everyday objects.

The fourth law is: "The lesson to be mastered must be explicable in the terms of truth already known by the learner—the unknown must be explained by means of the known."

Gregory points to the obvious fact that "our pupils learn the new by the aid of the old and familiar."[6] The known and familiar are *what give the lesson traction*. Otherwise, the words being used are just place-holders.

This law points to the importance of all the lessons of a course being connected in some kind of order that accumulates. The law is most often obeyed in subjects such as math, but commonly disregarded in subjects such as literature where books are often thrown at students willy-nilly. This law also points to the importance of a well-planned curriculum for the entire school. Every teacher should be able to assume certain kinds of knowledge on the part of the students and take that as a starting point for what needs to be taught next. A fifth grade teacher, for example, should know what her students learned in the fourth grade, and that information *should be helpful to her.*

The fifth law is that "teaching is arousing and uses the pupil's mind to grasp the desired thought or to master the desired art."

We have to be careful with this law, because we are prone to think that it means entertaining students instead of teaching them. Gregory says, "Excite and direct the self-activities of the pupil, and as a rule tell him nothing that he can learn himself."[7] This means work on the part of the pupil. The entertainment model goes in the opposite direction. When the student is entertained rather than taught, he is in an oxymoronic way being *aroused to passivity*. Good teaching awakens in the student a desire to learn. Gregory again: "True teaching, then, is not that which gives knowledge, but that which stimulates pupils to gain it."[8]

When students exhibit a "will-that-be-on-the-test?" kind of smarts, they are confessing that they have simply loaded a pile of facts (not necessarily understood) into temporary memory, to be off-loaded again whenever it is academically safe to do so. We must remember that "knowing comes by thinking, not by being told."[9]

The sixth law teaches that "learning is thinking into one's own understanding a new idea or truth or working into habit a new art or skill."

In Gregory's words, "The pupil must reproduce in his own mind the truth to be learned." He must turn it over in his own hands. Gregory chastises those who think that learning is the same thing as verbatim recital.[10] He is not criticizing catechism learning, but those who think that memorizing certain answers is *anything other than a first step in learning* the material. Repeating a catechism answer is at the grammar stage of catechism, not the rhetoric stage.

Gregory says that the "failure to insist upon original thinking by the pupils is one of the most common faults of our schools."[11] This is particularly true of modern Christian schools, which are prone to think of any probing question on the part of the student as an assault on orthodoxy.

The seventh law says this: "The test and proof of teaching done—the finishing and fastening process—must be a reviewing, rethinking, reknowing, reproducing, and applying of the material that has been taught, the knowledge and ideals and arts that have been communicated."

One of the reasons why bitter people have such good memories of the events that embittered them is related (in a weird, twisted fashion) to this principle. Review, review, review makes every detail sharp.

Imparting the ability to retain knowledge over time is one of the great tasks of education, and it is important for the teacher to help the students learn how to do this. This principle is not honored simply by having a monster test, all of it cumulative. Like every other aspect of teaching, the reviewing should be thoughtful, orderly, systematic, and cumulative.

In conclusion, violation of these laws is sometimes the best teacher of them. Who has not suffered under a teacher who did not know what he was talking about? Who as a student has not misspent hours in a classroom, not gathering anything? Who has not been at some point lost because no one was defining terms? Who has not been wearied by a droning refusal of a teacher to try to interest anyone in the subject? Who has not memorized something for a test and then promptly forgotten it? And who has not lost forever something that could have been readily retained by just a little thoughtful review?

24

ALTERNATIVES TO SCHOOL

WHEN I FIRST WROTE *Recovering the Lost Tools of Learning*, home-schooling was just beginning to make the national scene. Ten years before that, when we were involved in starting Logos School, I am not sure that I had even heard of homeschooling. One of the reasons for writing this book is that in the ten years since *Recovering*, the educational landscape has altered drastically.

We have seen an explosion of homeschooling and multiple combinations of homeschooling with other educational services. "According to a new federal report, at least 850,000 students were learning at home in 1999, the most recent year studied; some experts believe the figure is actually twice that."[1] Many of these students are being taught at home by their parents. Some of them are involved in Internet tutorials. Many are enrolled in correspondence academies. When it comes to homeschooling and its environs, recent years have seen the development of many free-market educational alternatives, which has brought about many blessings. If one throws the burgeoning Christian school movement into the mix, the circumstances are completely different from what they were in the late seventies when I first began to think seriously about education.

During this time the homeschooling movement has contributed many valuable things to our understanding of education. First, home-schoolers have demonstrated in a clear way that *parents* are responsible for the education of their children. Second, such parents have frequently demonstrated the degree of dedication necessary for a godly education to take place. Some parents have gone to jail; others have had to live and teach in the shadow of an overweening state, and, of course, there are the regular day-in, day-out demands of teaching your children.

At the same time, despite everything that has happened in the last twenty years, I think the basic issues are unchanged. The writer of Ecclesiastes said that under the sun there is nothing new. Things do not really change the way moderns like to pretend they do. And this is why this book has been written with the assumed setting of a Christian class-room in mind, a setting I prefer and have spent many years encouraging.

I want to defend the Christian classroom as a normal and appropri-ate way to teach children, one that has been used for millennia by covenant parents and that should not be rejected for modern ideological reasons. Covenant schools were common before the time of Christ. The classroom can (and often should) be rejected for *practical* reasons, but that is another thing entirely.

By no means is this chapter intended as a sweeping criticism of homeschooling, because I do believe it is frequently an appropriate way to teach children. The criticism is directed at educational ideologues of whatever stripe—whether the ideologues demand classical academies or rigid homeschooling. The chief characteristic of this kind of ideology is the assumption that fulfillment of the "ideological mandate," whatever that mandate might be, will usher in the next age of peace and glory. But this belief treats an educational method as though it is a savior, instead of a service to be offered up to our Savior.

We tend to bond to all the wrong things. Picture a four-lane highway, two lanes headed to heaven and two lanes to hell. Alongside one another, a Ford and a Chevy are driving to heaven, and on the other side of the road a Ford and a Chevy are heading the other way. If the guy in the heaven-bound Ford beeps and waves at the other Ford and periodically glares at the guy in the Chevy headed the same direction he is, his pri-orities are seriously skewed.

I know homeschoolers who have far more in common with our school philosophy than they have with other homeschoolers. And I know parents whose mind-set is entirely alien to mine, and yet they have their children enrolled in classical Christian schools. We must always emphasize the principle and not the particular method employed to ful-fill the principle. I'm not attacking methods here—methods are always necessary. Nor am I proclaiming methodological egalitarianism, as though every method were automatically equal, as though every car driv-ing in the right direction must drive equally well.

An ideologue can be identified by language or demeanor that shows that deep down he does not believe it is *possible* to drive a Ford to hell. I have no problem in saying that there are many Christian schools that are horrible places to enroll a child and that there are classical Christian academies out there that would make me a homeschooler. There are good Christian schools, and there are poor ones. In the same way, there are fantastic homeschools, and there are also wretched homeschools. I remember a poem my mother used to recite when I was a boy: There once was a girl "who had a curl right in the middle of her forehead. When she was good, she was very, very good, and when she was bad, she was horrid."

An ideologue says that a homeschool is good by definition. I call such ideologues *homers*. Or perhaps an ideologue says that a classical Christian school is good by definition. But Jesus taught us to look to fruit, not profession—deeds, not words.

Now the differing methods employed by classroom educators and home educators *will* likely mean that if they go wrong, they will go wrong in different ways. A Christian school is obviously more likely to suffer from the temptations of administrative bureaucracy. A homeschool is more like to suffer the temptation of allowing an undisciplined, nonacademic atmosphere to take over—and so on.

So I say all these things as a friend of homeschoolers who are doing what God calls them to do. I have sought to do whatever I can do to help encourage them in their God-appointed tasks. I have also written to encourage homeschoolers who want to employ the classical approach to their homeschool situation.[2] When it comes to support for dedicated homeschooling, I am a pal and a buddy. Nevertheless, I know that some readers are braced for the next word—*but*.

But I do have some concerns. These concerns are presented as a small offering to what I hope becomes a more general discussion. In an educational free market, intelligent decisions cannot be made without open discussion of the options. In saying what I do, I am not concerned about offending those who would be offended at anything less than complete agreement. But I *am* concerned about offending homeschoolers who are not ideologically driven, who are careful to guard against presumption, and who are discharging their responsibilities faithfully. Have I qualified myself enough? No, not really.

I am not saying these things as a stranger to the issues, as an outsider unfamiliar with homeschooling. Since the publication of *Recovering*, I have also been privileged to be part of establishing New St. Andrews College. This school has given me the opportunity to teach and get to know students from all over the country, many of them homeschooled. As part of the admissions process, I have reviewed the academic achievements of many of them. As a pastor, I have also been involved in providing counsel to families that have chosen homeschooling and have dealt with some of the significant pastoral issues that can arise both in school and homeschool settings.

This said, homeschoolers who are employing the classical model should guard themselves in three key areas. If there is a problem in any one of these areas, the solution is not necessarily to "cease homeschooling." But a solution does depend on more than simply wanting the problems to fix themselves.

Some homeschoolers have not allotted a sufficient amount of time for the process of classical education. Despite what many claim, it is *not* possible to do in two or three hours what it takes people in a classroom eight hours to do. Then, too, the resources of time and energy are sometimes not given to the work. It is not possible to get a classical education "to go." Parents who do not have prep time can sometimes expect the texts to do all the teaching. But one of the glories of education is the opportunity to hear the truth come out of a human being with blood in the veins and air in the lungs, and not just off a printed page.

Sometimes homeschooled children who have learned to read are turned loose on all the books in the house and the local library. They are fierce readers, and by the time they are fourteen, they have read everything. But the danger is that their education can become little more than reading. When they come to take their SATs, they discover that their verbal scores are stratospheric, and their math scores give the impression that the test was taken by a rock that was having trouble holding the pencil.

A second problem is familism. Many homeschooling families are quite large. In this setting, sometimes a tight familism takes over, and the families seek to become self-sufficient in all things. As a result they may become detached from the larger community. Pretty soon everything is being done at home—medicine, church, college education, and so on. But we are not called to a hermitage of the family.

Sometimes practical problems can be created by larger families. The younger children are short-changed in their education because the parents are just plain *weary* by the time their turn comes, or parents are too busy trying to keep up with the older children. This problem might be called the snapshot phenomenon. The firstborn child often has multitudes of photographs taken of him, but the fifth child might have a hard time figuring out what he looked like when he was a kid. There are homeschooling parents who excelled with their older children, but the younger kids do not receive nearly the same amount of educational attention.

A different problem can also occur in larger families, particularly when some of the older children are girls. As the family grows, mother needs more and more help, and sometimes the older girls become surrogate mothers. These girls have to forego their studies in order to help with the little ones. This situation can be justified by saying the girls are learning to be domestic, which they are. But they ought not to learn domesticity at the expense of the rest of their education.

The third problem is related to the sex of the child. Girls who are being homeschooled are growing up in an environment for which they are suited and being prepared. But boys are called by God to go out into the world. A wise father needs to watch his daughters closely if they are enrolled in a school—girls can become detached from their homes in an unfortunate way. But, as I stated in *Future Men*, a wise father should also watch a homeschooled son.[3] He can become *attached* to the home in an unfortunate way—one boy among sisters, taught by Mom.

With all this said, homeschooling can generally work better prior to third grade with one or two kids. In many situations, parents of such children can outperform a good school. But as age and numbers of children increase, the schools do have the advantage of the division of labor and generally can do a better job. Some people are renaissance parents, of course, and do a wonderful job all the way through.

But even here, when children are enrolled in a school, the school is not an adequate substitute for the parents. Rather, the school should be thought of as a pedagogical servant. Whether the teaching is happening in the classroom or around the kitchen table, *both* parents must always be active and involved in the education of their children.

25

THE THREAT OF STATE ENTANGLEMENT

AS A MATTER OF POLICY, the Association of Classical and Christian Schools requires its member schools that desire accreditation with ACCS to refrain from accepting vouchers. Such a stand can be confusing, because it is usually the left-wing education establishment that opposes vouchers, and conservative Christian groups frequently support them. So why this stand?

A voucher should be understood as a monetary payment made to parents of school-age children by any agency of the civil government in the United States, whether federal, state, or local. That money is to be used for tuition or tuition assistance in a private academy. This definition covers many voucher plans being proposed but does not cover other educational option plans, such as various tax credit proposals. Some creative plans are being proposed that do not create the same problem vouchers do. For example, Martin Angell, founder in Texas of A Choice for Every Child Foundation, is a leader in the work of establishing a private foundation that provides tuition assistance to needy children. The only role of the government is to give a tax credit to those who donate to the foundation. The foundation in turn helps to provide needy families with an educational choice. The families that receive assistance can attend a school that is not subject to any government control.[1]

But vouchers are a different story. The issue here is one of ultimate religious authority in our schools. It is not a concern about the proper relationship of the civil magistrate to a Christian school in an (ideal) Christian republic. Thus the difficulty is not over the abstract question of "school and state" in an ideal setting. One could argue, for example, that in a Christian republic there would be no problem with civil support for schools. That issue would provide material for an interesting utopian debate, but it has little to do with the voucher proposals that we have to deal with today.

Our concern is far more particular. Every civil government in the United States is prohibited by law from acknowledging the lordship of Jesus Christ in any way. Christian schools, on the other hand, are seeking to acknowledge the authority of the Lord Jesus in every area of life. These positions are irreconcilable.

My concern over vouchers is that we do not want our schools funded by those who have shown themselves to be formally antagonistic to everything we are trying to do and teach. Someone might respond that Scripture allows for "plundering the Egyptians" and that the use of vouchers is just a modern-day example of this. The difficulty with this view is that the Egyptians are not being plundered—we are. We are not a victorious people being led by our God away from the smoldering ruin that once was Egypt. Right now we are still settled in Babylon, and the Babylonian rulers have seen that our schools are pretty good. They want a piece of the action and are willing to pay for it. The tragedy is that many Christian education activists are starting to dicker about the price.

In my view, the acceptance of vouchers would be a significant first step in bringing our Christian schools under the direct control of an unbelieving civil magistrate. One proverb expresses the principle well: He who takes the king's coin becomes the king's man. If we receive money from the government, we must know that the money comes with conditions. Today the conditions might be tolerable. In fact, they will certainly be tolerable because otherwise the bait would not hide the hook. But if they are not tolerable tomorrow—for example, if the rules change so that schools receiving such vouchers may not discriminate on the basis of sexual orientation—we will discover that getting out of the trap is a lot more difficult than getting into it.

Our unbelieving government will argue (rightly) that our receipt of their money meant that we must conform to the public policy of the civil government. They have already successfully argued this way. In the famous Bob Jones case, argued before the Supreme Court, the benefit of a tax exemption meant that Bob Jones could not have a dating policy that was contrary to the policy of the federal government. The fact that the policy at Bob Jones was an unbiblical one is beside the point. In a *free* country, they would have had the right to be silly. Consequently, our current legal situation is such that institutions that receive money from the government had better be prepared to receive their overall marching orders from that same government.

One might argue that if the government started requiring the hiring of homosexual teachers, then the school could decline the vouchers at that point. But this suggestion ignores the nature of institutional and budgetary growth. It is possible that some schools would decline vouchers. But if the budget has expanded to accommodate the new voucher money, it will be very difficult for the school to return to its original size without firing staff, closing programs, dismissing a third of the student body, etc. In other words, there will be a great deal of immediate and practical pressure to capitulate.

Our stand on vouchers is not being urged in a perfectionist fashion. We understand that children will be driven to our schools on roads paid for by this secular government. They will all have various entanglements with government money, whether it is parents on Medicare, surplus cheese in their lunch bags, or participation in parks and recreational athletic programs. My concern is not to have every minor problem fixed instantly; rather, it is to avoid creating a new, significant entanglement that would bring our schools under the authority of those who refuse to acknowledge our Lord.

True, the fact that such things could happen does not mean they necessarily would. But in the instances where they have happened, often the school set itself up for the problem and in effect *invited* the problem. In other words, the disaster need not be universal to be significant. We would be grateful for those instances where a school has escaped losing its academic freedom. Occasionally, a school will not reap what it sows. But as a general pattern, it remains true that God is not mocked. If we sow government involvement, we must not be surprised at the (now unwanted) government involvement at harvesttime.

We are seeking the freedom to teach our students that the lordship of Christ is relevant in all that they do. One of the best things we can do in this regard is to set an example for them. The all-encompassing lordship of Christ should affect how we decide to fund our schools and in this case how we have determined not to fund them.

We have not yet learned what liberty is. Nathan Wilson points out the problem with moving from one unbelieving economic system to another as a way of funding our schools:

> The government school system is failing as it is. Vouchers could tip the entire current system over the brink into oblivion more quickly, but that's where the government schools are going anyway. Vouchers hasten the demise of the current statism, but also hasten the advent of a new kind of educational statism. Socialism is when the government owns the industry in question. Fascism is when the industry is privately owned, but controlled by the government. Although they do not understand it this way, proponents of vouchers want the socialist schools to fall . . . so that we may have fascist schools. And Christians have not yet gotten to the point where they want liberty in education.[2]

A Proposed Curriculum

26

TURNING IT AROUND:
A THOUGHT EXPERIMENT

"KING FOR A DAY" thought experiments are challenging, rewarding, and dangerous. The challenge is that it can be difficult to think through any situation with all the current variables removed. Such experiments are rewarding because if they are conducted with an appropriate level of sobriety, they can be a tremendous help in clarifying vision. "What would you do if everyone let you?" is actually the same question as "what are you actually trying to accomplish?" But such thought experiments are dangerous because they require that we postulate a frictionless world, which is not the world we live in. Thus it is all too easy to drift off into utopian speculations. And having just escaped from the twentieth century, who needs those anymore?

That said, and with appropriate caveats issued, what course should we set in order to "turn education around"? Our hypothetical situation is this: Suppose we are dealing with a fairly large Christian school (five hundred students or so, K-12). The board has decided that they are adrift and lacking in vision. The parents are in complete agreement with this assessment, without one dissenting voice. They have asked me to present a series of reforms to them, and what I say they will do. Moreover, I have good reason to believe that they will actually do it. The student council at their last gathering decided that everyone is tired of sneakers and blue jeans and that fifteen minutes of homework a night is too little. Students want a change too. And in addition, *mirabile dictu*, all the reforms I have in mind do not violate any existing federal or state laws or UN declarations on human rights. Now what?

As I present my suggested reforms to this school, I do not at all assume that *everything* they are doing is currently wrong. Many of their course offerings should be retained, with higher standards in them the only change. They should keep their algebra courses, albeit somewhat beefed up.

First are the foundational issues. The school needs to acquire a confessional identity. When we consider what we are up against, a broad and generic evangelical approach availeth not. Consequently, two things are necessary. The first is that the school must adopt a confession of faith in line with the confessional commitments of historic and classical Protestantism. Pop evangelical sentiments, diffused in their normal gaseous way, are utterly inadequate for resisting the spirit of *our* age, which wants to seep into the unsuspecting school through every available crack. The second aspect of this needed confessional integrity is that the school would be supported by one or more churches in the area that share the same reformational zeal and are willing to preach, teach, administer the sacraments, and discipline in terms of that zeal. Apart from reformation in the church, reformation in anything else, especially in schools, will come to *nada, zilch.*

The second foundational task would be to make a genuine countercultural statement in the transformed appearance of the student body. The students would all be required to wear uniforms or defined school clothing, and all forms of cultural outlandishness would be banished from the premises. Gone, but not missed, would be purple hair, body piercings, baggy pants, portable CD players, tattoos, along with every other form of pop culture that enables young people today to slouch around looking disgruntled. It is not that every form of popular culture is evil (it is not), but pop culture generally *is* a distraction from the work of classical and Christian education. The fact that much of the banished *kultursmog* is sinful simply provides an added bonus.

Third, I would raise tuition so that at least 85 percent of the cost of the education was paid by the parents. The remainder would be covered by the school's very capable development office. The teachers in our school would be paid at a significantly higher rate than most teachers in Christian schools. At the same time, we would not take the salary schedules of the government schools as the normative standard. The teachers there have lost a tremendous amount of vocational prestige because of their unionizing approach. The laborer *is* truly worthy of his hire, but at the same time, honor and respect in the community are a large part of the intangible rewards teachers have traditionally received. I would want our teachers to be highly respected, paid decently, and at the same time not to be dismissed by the public as mere hirelings.

Fourth, I would want to keep the school free of all governmental entanglements. Tax support for education is not inherently wrong; in fact, it might be defensible if our government were openly Christian. But I would stay away from such entanglements because our current government is pluralistic (the theological name for this being polytheism). Because of this, I do not trust them to keep their alien faith from interfering with the Christian faith we are seeking to promote in our school. I would steer clear of all government-aid patronage packages for education that could be categorized in the voucher category.

Once the foundational issues were established and the concrete dry, I would turn to the curriculum. The structure I would propose is that of the medieval Trivium, as developed and applied by Dorothy Sayers. She noted that children grow naturally through three stages, each one corresponding to an element of that Trivium, which consists of grammar, dialectic, and rhetoric.

In the elementary years generally, the students go through what she called the Poll-parrot stage. They love to chant, memorize, and recite. If they are not given things to chant, memorize, and recite, they will make up their own. This activity corresponds to the grammar stage of the Trivium. At this point in their education, the kids would memorize vast amounts of information—presidents, kings, mountain ranges, rivers, multiplication tables, battles, catechism answers, psalms, and so forth. Here the school is cutting with the grain. The children enjoy taking large amounts of information on, and so we will gladly accommodate them. They do not yet have it all sorted out, which is fine. That will come at the next stage.

From this point, they grow into what Miss Sayers called the Pert stage. This stage matches the dialectic phase of the Trivium. At this point children begin to question and dispute. They wonder why they are being made to learn all this stuff. They wonder why they can't listen to a portable CD player during lunch hour. They wonder why, how, and how come? They develop a natural disposition to argue, and so, continuing to cut with the grain, we teach them to argue. So they will take a course in symbolic logic and argumentation in the eighth grade. In their other courses, they are learning to relate all the various facts they have already accumulated. This stage corresponds generally to the junior high years.

They then come to the Poetic stage in their high school years, which corresponds to the rhetoric stage of the Trivium. At this age young people are very concerned with their appearance—how they are coming across. Consequently, now the school will teach them how to present themselves in a rhetorically winsome way. They will take rhetoric during these years, along with all their literature courses. In Bible class they will take apologetics. Instead of a prom, they will be trained in manners and etiquette in preparation for various "protocol nights" where they attend different cultural events as a class—dinner at a classy restaurant and then a night at the opera.

But I am afraid I would be unsatisfied with this mere skeleton of the Trivium. I would want some "fat on these bones," much more than what is available in many of our traditional course offerings. As such additions are considered, we run into the old how-many-hours-we-have-in-the-day problem, but there is nothing here that cannot be dealt with in principle.

I would begin instruction in Latin no later than the third grade. Once the Latin instruction has begun, all students would take Latin through the tenth grade. At this time, they would have the option of continuing their Latin for two more years or of switching to Greek or Hebrew for their junior and senior years.

I would require that all students acquire musical literacy. There would be at a minimum half an hour of musical instruction a day, and this instruction would include sight-reading, choral participation, and working with basic instruments. The students, once musically literate, would be taught to sing through the vast library of psalms, hymns, and great choral music that is an essential part of the church's heritage.

Particularly in the older grades, I would want to integrate the subjects they are studying as much as possible. For example, they should be taking classical literature the same year they are taking ancient history and Old Testament survey. In another year, they should take American history, American literature, and civics together. Such integration prods them into thinking, not just in the classrooms, but also in the hallways.

Something must be said about instruction in phonics. Although many Christian schools do instruct their little ones to read by a phonetic method, the "whole language" approach has still had a corrupting influence. I would want to ensure that all the teachers who teach reading in the lower levels are purists on the question of phonics and that no student would leave the first grade without knowing how to read.

I would *increase* the number of particular extracurricular activities and would dramatically raise the GPA requirement to participate in any of them. These activities would include things such as drama, choir, and athletics. The GPA required for participation would be 3.0. Thus all participants in such activities would be student scholars. They would find that these activities, far from discouraging their central interest in academics, would be a great stimulus and encouragement to them in their academic calling. True discipline in one area always flows into others.

Such educational experiments, conducted in the airy regions of the mind, have to end sometime. The daydream ends, and we look around sadly, wondering if the thing is possible. Certainly it is not possible to accomplish such things in an easy and frictionless way. But it can be done and has been done. Numerous schools around the country really are undertaking this work. And when the thing is accomplished on the ground, in the real world, overcoming unbelief and apathy, the gratitude and satisfaction are beyond words.

27

CANONICAL BOOKS

A FAVORITE REVIEWING exercise is to ask someone what book they would take with them onto a desert island. G. K. Chesterton once answered this question by saying that he would take a guide to shipbuilding. There are also the obvious "right" answers—the Bible—and other answers calculated to play to the gallery.

I propose to allow myself a little more scope. I want to list twenty-five books that should be found somewhere in the curriculum of a classical Christian school. These books should be read and studied at some point in the course of a student's time in a classical Christian school and college. Of course, the point of such a list is not to get all of classical education into one cardboard box, but rather to show what kind of books would go into such a selection. Such a list might be helpful also for those who want to establish a classical Christian school, but who are wary about trying to provide an education they did not receive. To read through such a list does not provide a classical education, obviously, but it does have the capacity to orient someone to what a classical education is about.[1]

This first list should be considered *foundational*—that is, it should be considered as basic to the task of classical Christian education, which is not the same thing as the *point* of classical Christian education. The foundations list is not the same thing as the fruition list. In plain terms, if I were to be stranded on a desert island and had a choice of twenty-five books to read for the rest of my days, the list below, with a handful of exceptions, would not be what I would take. At the conclusion of this chapter, I will include a list of twenty-five books that, in my view, represent the fruit of our cultural heritage and that would provide a decent library for the stranded.

The list below should form an important part of a classical and Christian education so that our children may go on to read and appreciate the many works of literature that have "stood on these shoulders" and may, Lord willing, eventually contribute to that growing body of literature themselves.

The Scriptures

Of course, the Scriptures are not included in the list of twenty-five books. The Bible is necessarily in a class by itself and forms the center of every class a student takes. But at the same time, the Bible is an important part of our broader literary heritage, particularly in the Authorized Version, popularly known as the King James. There are many issues involved here, but I do not believe a classical Christian education should revolve around *The Skateboarder's Study Bible.*[2]

The Iliad

Written by Homer (c. 750 B.C.), this great work is about the fall of Hector in one sense, as well as the tragic fall of Achilles during the siege of Troy. The Trojan War is the setting, but this is not what *The Iliad* is about. Homer's poetic gifts were great, but we should remember C. S. Lewis's comment that it was his giftedness that made his granite despair shine as though it were marble.

The Odyssey

Mark Twain once quipped that we now know that Homer was not the author of these works, but they were rather to be attributed to another blind Greek poet with the same name. *The Odyssey*, more accessible to many modern readers than *The Iliad*, is about the return of Odysseus from a life of freebooting to his home country and his adventures on the way.

The Oresteia

Aeschylus was the father of Greek tragedy (525-456 B.C.). The *Oresteia* is a trilogy of three plays (458 B.C.)—*Agamemnon, The Libation Bearers* (*Choephoroe*), and *The Kindly Ones* (*Eumenides*). The apostle Paul's language indicates his familiarity with these plays. The plays are about the return of Agamemnon from the Trojan War, his murder by his wife, and the unraveling of his dynastic order followed by the rise of another, more balanced order.

History of the Persian Wars

Herodotus (484-c. 424 B.C.) was a great storyteller. He was first called the father of history by Cicero, but the appellation has stuck. Modernist historians want to qualify this somewhat, thinking that he has insufficient quantified boredom in his footnotes to be called a true historian. Nonetheless, he is a lot of fun to read.

Oedipus Rex

Sophocles (c. 497-406 B.C.) wrote this play about a man fated to kill his own father and marry his mother. Aristotle used the play as his model for tragedy, and it has had a great influence on the definition of tragedy. *Oedipus Rex* also serves as a good springboard for discussions about fate and free will.

The Republic

Plato (c. 428-c. 347 B.C.) was great because he raised great issues. Of course, he also answered them from within his pagan worldview. This book should be read because it is important in the history of ideas, not because the ideas therein represent anything that Christians would want to adopt. Karl Marx was an intellectual who suffered misfortune because people tried to put his ideas into practice. Had Plato suffered the same misfortune, the world would still be talking about that totalitarian hellhole.

Nicomachean Ethics

As Plato's greatest student, Aristotle (384-322 B.C.) served as a tutor for Alexander the Great. His *Nicomachean Ethics* has had a major influence in Western moral philosophy, much of it problematic for the Christian. The pernicious influence comes more from the basis of the standard (reason versus revelation) than it does from what Aristotle praises or blames. When Paul asks, "Where is the wise man?" he is almost certainly talking about Aristotle. Man through all his knowing does not know God.

The Aeneid

Virgil (70-19 B.C.) was the court poet for Augustus, the Caesar when Jesus was born. He retold the story of the founding of Rome, connecting it to the fall of Troy. Trojan refugees fled after the fall of their city, and after many adventures, they settled in Italy. Aeneas, their leader, is a man in the first part of the *Aeneid*, but as the poem progresses, he becomes a personification of Rome itself.

On the Incarnation

Athanasius (A.D. 295-373), the bishop of Alexandria, was the orthodox champion against the heresies of Arius, who denied the deity of Christ. The testimony of C. S. Lewis on this point should be sufficient: "When I first opened his *De Incarnatione*, I soon discovered by a very simple test that I was reading a masterpiece."[3]

The Confessions of St. Augustine

Augustine (A.D. 354-430) was one of the greatest thinkers the church has ever produced, and it would be hard to overstate his influence. His *Confessions* are autobiographical, devotional, philosophical, and everywhere rich. The Protestant Reformation should really be understood as Augustinian Christianity coming into its own, and Protestants would do well to get reacquainted with their spiritual father.

Beowulf

The author was an unknown Christian poet from the eighth century (c. A.D. 700-750). The story is of a great hero who slays the monsters Grendel and Grendel's mother, and who at the end of the epic lays down his life for his people in a fight with a dragon. This is a wonderful poem.

The Divine Comedy

In this work many believe that Dante (A.D. 1265-1321) produced the supreme Christian literary work. Throughout the course of this "sacred poem," Dante as pilgrim is escorted through Hell, Purgatory, and Heaven, and comes finally to the Beatific Vision.

The Canterbury Tales

Geoffrey Chaucer (A.D. 1343-1400) belongs to the high medieval period. His greatness as a poet is generally recognized. Pilgrims on the way to Canterbury tell one another stories to pass the time, and the stories reveal many of the tensions and contradictions of medieval life—from sacred to profane, from holy to bawdy. With regard to the bawdy aspect, Chaucer himself believed that he sometimes got carried away, and much to the consternation of modern liberated scholars, he said he was sorry. Chaucer was almost certainly influenced by his contemporary, Wycliffe, and was probably numbered among the Lollards, followers of Wycliffe.

Hamlet, Macbeth, Henry V, Much Ado About Nothing, Midsummer Night's Dream

William Shakespeare presents us with some difficulties. The first is the question of dates, which depend on who Shakespeare was. Since I follow Joseph Sobran's arguments for the Oxfordian authorship of the plays, I simply refer you to him.[4] The other difficulty is that of selecting which plays should represent his genius, whoever he was. The five above will have to do. Since they are plays, they were meant to be seen, not read. Good videos of some of these are available.

Institutes of the Christian Religion

John Calvin (1509-1564) was a strong personality who still evokes strong and sometimes passionate responses, both for and against. Nevertheless, the stubborn historical fact remains that he was the single greatest systematizer and organizer of the Protestant theology and faith. He was a truly great man, and this great work was published in its first form when Calvin was still a young man.

Vindicae Contra Tyrannos

Junius Brutus is a pseudonym for an unknown Huguenot writer of the sixteenth century. This book represents a Protestant marriage of medieval and modern thinking about political civil order. The book was enormously influential in the American colonies prior to our War for Independence.

The Temple

George Herbert (1593-1633) was a devotional Anglican poet whose great theme was the authority of grace. Like his contemporary John Donne, he was a poetic craftsman of the first order. The catholicity of his writing has given him a broad appeal among Christians.

Paradise Lost

John Milton (1608-1674) was a genius of the first rank. One astute observer said that the English language collapsed under the weight of that genius. *Paradise Lost* is an artistic monument, but it is not an easy one to apprehend at a first reading. Taking a class on it or reading some companion volumes would be very helpful.[5]

Pilgrim's Progress

John Bunyan (1628-1688) was an unlettered tinker turned preacher who wrote a book that continues to astonish the world. The allegory is straightforward, but the book nevertheless has depths that account for its incredible staying power. C. S. Lewis said of this work: "The greater part of it is enthralling narrative or genuinely dramatic dialogue. Bunyan stands with Malory and Trollope as a master of perfect naturalness in the mimesis of ordinary conversation. . . . In dialogue Bunyan catches not only the cadence of the speech but the tiny twists of thought."[6]

Pensees

Blaise Pascal (1623-1662) was a Jansenist, part of a movement within the post-Reformation Roman Catholic Church trying to turn Rome back to an Augustinian foundation. The Jansenists are best understood as "Protestants" who never left the Church of Rome. Pascal was a great mathematical genius as well as a devotional mystic. "The heart has its reasons of which reason knows nothing: we know this in countless ways."

Pride and Prejudice

Jane Austen (1775-1817) wrote one of the finest examples of a comedy of manners. Her writing displays an understanding of great psychological depths without becoming pathological about it, as more recent writers have done.

Faust

Johann Goethe (1749-1832) created in this drama a work that is archetypical of the great Romantic themes of his era. Many German legends told fantastic stories of the fifteenth-century magician Georg

Faust, who sold his soul to the devil. Christopher Marlowe wrote a play about Faust in the late sixteenth century, at the end of which the soul of Faustus is lost. Goethe ends the story differently, and in that difference we can see the desolations of our modern era. Instead of salvation by grace, we have salvation for free.

The Adventures of Huckleberry Finn

Mark Twain published this book in 1885. The fact that just about everyone reads it in high school and that it is a really good story enjoyed on the surface tends to obscure for us just what a *great* book it is. Hemingway said that all modern literature descends from *Huckleberry Finn*. H. L. Mencken praised Twain to the heights.

The Brothers Karamazov

This novel by Fyodor Dostoyevsky (1821-1881) is in the minds of many one of the contenders for the title of the greatest novel ever written. This is a strange way to talk about a novel, too reminiscent of *People* magazine's tendency to declare someone or other the sexiest man alive. Nevertheless, this kind of praise does give some idea of the novel's reputation, and it is fair to say that it represents "a consummate work of Christian imagination."[7]

The Lord of the Rings

J. R. R. Tolkien (1892-1973) wrote what is already being called *the* novel of the twentieth century. While it is far too early to make this judgment, it is certainly not too early to hope that the judgment proves correct. The story of the one ring, of Frodo, Sam, Gandalf, and every other creature in Middle Earth will no doubt be read for centuries to come.

Those who read through this list will certainly get an introductory orientation to the world of classical literature. While many treasures are on the list, as mentioned before, this list does not represent the fruition of *belles lettres* as understood from a classical Christian framework. And here is the value of the true desert-island test. If I were going to be stranded on a desert island for the rest of my life and, besides the Bible, had to limit myself to twenty-five books, what would they be? Almost half the books from the first list make it to the second, but they are still a minority. The remainder are perhaps a little too revealing, but here goes.

The Odyssey—Homer
History of the Persian Wars—Herodotus
The Aeneid—Virgil
The Works of Josephus—Josephus
On the Incarnation—Athanasius
City of God—Augustine
Beowulf—unknown
Hamlet, Macbeth, Henry V, Much Ado About Nothing, Midsummer Night's Dream—William Shakespeare
Bondage of the Will—Martin Luther
Institutes of the Christian Religion—John Calvin
The Temple—George Herbert
Pilgrim's Progress—John Bunyan
Method for Prayer—Matthew Henry
Book of Common Prayer—Thomas Cranmer
Pride and Prejudice—Jane Austen
The Adventures of Huckleberry Finn—Mark Twain
A Treasury of David—Charles Spurgeon
Orthodoxy—G. K. Chesterton
Chronicles of Narnia —C. S. Lewis
The Screwtape Letters—C. S. Lewis
The Lord of the Rings—J. R. R. Tolkien
A Mencken Chrestomathy—H. L. Mencken
The World of Mulliner—P. G. Wodehouse
Oxford Book of English Verse—Arthur Quiller-Couch
The American Heritage Dictionary

And if any young men came to see me in my Robinson Crusoe tree-fort library about my daughter, I would be quite at leisure.

THE DAWN OF
EVERLASTING RESULTS

28

AND UNTO CHILDREN'S CHILDREN

EDUCATION DOES NOT occur in a vacuum. It is a central part of child rearing, and broadly understood with the *paideia* of God in mind, it *is* child rearing. Christian childrearing does not occur outside the context of God's promises. I still believe that "it is a tragedy of monumental proportions that most modern Christian parents are not aware of the wonderful promises that God has made in His Word on the subject of child rearing."[1]

Promises are given to believing parents so that they might believe them, not so that they might work to earn them. All God's promises are from grace, through grace, and unto grace. We respond to His grace, the Bible teaches, with faith. Further, quoting from *Standing on the Promises*, I maintain that "the Scriptures are equally clear that the heart of covenant-keeping is promise-believing. This is why the Bible, from beginning to end, teaches the centrality of faith."[2]

In Deuteronomy 6, Moses begins his exposition of the Ten Commandments, starting appropriately enough with the first commandment. "Now these are the commandments, the statutes, and the judgments, which the LORD your God commanded to teach you, that ye might do them in the land whither ye go to possess it" (Deut. 6:1). God has given the people a commandment, statutes, and judgments, and Moses delivers these along with instruction (v. 1). The intent behind the instruction is obedience in the land. A right obedience proceeds from a fear of God extended over generations so that blessing might follow (v. 2). Israel is to hear and do, that they may "increase mightily" in a land of profound blessings (v. 3). Then follows the *Shema* (vv. 4-9), Israel's great confession of faith and vow of loving obedience. Jehovah is One (v. 4). He is to be loved with all that a person has and is (v. 5). The law is to be at the heart (v. 6). This love, this law—same thing—is to be manifested in the diligent and constant instruction of children (v. 7). The word is to be bound on the forehead or hand (v. 8) and written upon the posts and gates (v. 9).

In our second verse, obedience proceeds from a right-minded fear of God. In the third, desire for blessing is the motivation for obedience. In verse 5 and following, love is the basis for obedience. Therefore, to understand the fear of the Lord rightly, learn to see that fear *as love hungering for blessing*. Fear of God is the beginning of all true wisdom (Ps. 111:10). Through the fear of the Lord we depart from evil (Prov. 16:6). True fear is not generated by human beings (Isa. 29:13). This fear has to inform all true worship.

Our God is a God who blesses sinners, and when He does, the temptation to forget Him is immediately whispering at our elbow. In the promised land the skies "rained down milk, and the rocks were filled with honey." This abundance was from the hand of the Lord, and it was available to the people when they obeyed Him. So we see that the key to material blessing is *not* found in the presence of natural resources. Some of the most poverty-stricken people in the world live in the midst of lush surroundings. The key is loving obedience to God.

At the center of it all is true orthodoxy. We do not begin with a certain concept of monotheism in order to learn how we are to understand Yhwh. Rather, our covenant Jehovah God defines for us what monotheism means. Monotheism is meaningless apart from Him. The *Shema* teaches us that God, our God, is One.

This truth relates directly to our children. Jesus Christ teaches us that this passage contains the greatest commandment ever delivered to men and women. And we see that the commandment is delivered in the context of *God requiring covenant education for covenant children*. Love for God that does not result in Christian education for Christian children is not love for Him at all.

This love for God's law involved hands, posts, and gates. Loving devotion to the law of God was to be an *individual* commitment—bound on the hand or head. It was also a *household* commitment—posted at the door of every home. And last, it was to be a *social, cultural, and political* commitment—written on the gates. This last item, unfortunately, shows the anemia of the modern church. Our doctrine always comes down to action, and that action reveals our true doctrine. We do not understand the relationship between fear, hunger, and love. Our great problem is that we do not want enough from God. Ironically, we content ourselves with our discontents in the wilderness when before us a promised land awaits. Why do we not want milk and honey? Why do we not see the demands of the covenant as milk and honey? Why do we *not* want to teach our children when the promises of God stand patiently alongside us?

Too often we do not teach our children because we have nothing to say. We have nothing to say because we do not know the Scriptures or the power of God.

If Christian parents have a duty to educate their children in the Christian religion, then the ground of this duty is their religion. The ground of Christian education cannot be pragmatism or reaction. Christian parents must educate their children because to do so is the will of God, and to refuse to do so is rebellion against Him. The Christian school is not a synthesis that arises out of clashing human opinions.

But whenever we talk about religious "duty," we must be careful lest we get tangled up in the law and gospel business. The *promise* precedes the law, Paul argues, and is the foundation for it. All duty must arise from the gratitude for redemption, and this includes the duty of educating our covenant children. But in order for this education to happen, those children must be considered as included in that redemption. They are not short heathen, boarding with Christian parents temporarily.

There should be no mistake: Christian parents have a religious duty and obligation to provide a Christian education for their children (Eph. 6:4). The *paideia* of God must be established. But this responsibility, found in the last three chapters of Ephesians, must be grounded (as everything in those chapters is) on the first three chapters. The first three chapters teach us the doctrine of Christ. There is absolutely nothing to *do* in the first three chapters. Paul gives us one indicative statement after another, and the only thing to do with an indicative statement is believe it or not. If a man says the door is closed, it is not a proper response to say you will close it right away. You can believe him or not when he says this, but you cannot obey him by closing the door. It is closed already.

The most important word in Ephesians is *gar*, which means *therefore*. This word is the hinge upon which the argument of the whole book turns. After three chapters of teaching us the foundational doctrines of the Christian faith, Paul then says *therefore* . . . respect your husbands, love your wives, *teach your children*, keep the unity of the Spirit. He has three chapters of duties and commands, all of which should be understood as "therefore commands." It is not enough to obey; we must *therefore* obey.

As Christian parents, we pray for God to deliver us from our adversaries in order "that our sons may be as plants grown up in their youth; that our daughters may be as corner stones, polished after the similitude of a palace" (Ps. 144:12). Faith looks to the future, and the future includes our children and *their* children.

This faith stands on God's promises. "Train up a child in the way he should go: and when he is old, he will not depart from it" (Prov. 22:6). A good deal of ingenuity has been expended upon this verse, but the plain meaning is still probably the best. The problem resides in the implicit *modus tollens*—what are we to say if a child *does* depart from his upbringing?

In Ephesians 6:1-3, Paul tells children to honor their parents. This is, he says, the first commandment with a promise. Not only is the promise still good, but it has been greatly expanded. No longer is it limited to the land of Israel, but it also includes the entire earth. How are children to know how this is to be done? The answer is found in verse 4, in the *paideia* of the Lord. Fathers are to bring up their children in the nurture and admonition of the Lord so that they will honor their parents, so that in turn it will be well with them, and they will live long in the earth.

In the Ten Commandments, God says that He visits the sins of idolatrous fathers to the third and fourth generations (Deut. 5:9). In contrast, He shows mercy to thousands who love Him and keep His commandments. Thousands of what? This does not refer to thousands of people; contextually it means thousands of generations. This is made evident two chapters later when Moses says, "Know therefore that the LORD thy God, he is God, the faithful God, which keepeth covenant and mercy with them that love him and keep his commandments to a thousand *generations*" (Deut. 7:9, emphasis mine).

Throughout all Scripture, God deals with His people generationally. For this reason Christian education is right at the heart of covenant faithfulness. Education is the process whereby we teach our children to love and fear God, or to hate and despise Him. In our official tax-funded, agnostic academies, that hatred is shown through *ignoring* Him.

Great promises are given to Christian parents in Scripture. But we must also take note of the proper recipients of the promises. The promises are given to parents, not to the state. Louis Berkhof is right on target:

> God's special revelation teaches us the same truth with even greater clarity. Negatively, it may be said that the Bible in speaking of the duties of the state never mentions the work of educating the children of the nation (cf. Exod. 18:22-26; Deut. 1:16, 17; Matt. 22:17-21; Rom. 13:1-7; 1 Pet. 2:13-15). It is a striking fact that even the Old Testament, in which God deals with the nation of Israel more than with the individuals that belong to it and consequently speaks primarily in national terms, always refers to or addresses the parents as the responsible educators of the children.[3]

When the state undertakes the work that is not theirs, there is no promised blessing, and they wrest control of education from those who *do* have the promise for faithful obedience.

We have already seen education as one of the central demands of the covenant. As noted earlier, when the human race received the greatest command, that of loving God with all that we have and are, it was in the context of education.

> *Hear, O Israel: The LORD our God is one LORD: And thou shalt love the LORD thy God with all thine heart, and with all thy soul, and with all thy might. And these words, which I command thee this day, shall be in thine heart: And thou shalt teach them diligently unto thy children, and shalt talk of them when thou sittest in thine house, and when thou walkest by the way, and when thou liest down, and when thou risest up. And thou shalt bind them for a sign upon thine hand, and they shall be as frontlets between thine eyes. And thou shalt write them upon the posts of thy house, and on thy gates. (Deut. 6:4-9)*

We see the same thing in Psalm 78:

> *For he established a testimony in Jacob, and appointed a law in Israel, which he commanded our fathers, that they should make them known to their children: That the generation to come might know them, even the children which should be born; who should arise and declare them to their children: That they might set their hope in God, and not forget the works of God, but keep his commandments: And might not be as their fathers, a stubborn and rebellious generation; a gener-*

ation that set not their heart aright, and whose spirit was not stedfast with God. (Ps. 78:5-8)

And it is with this Old Testament background that Christian fathers are told to "provoke not your children to wrath: but bring them up in the nurture and admonition of the Lord" (Eph. 6:4). But we are to remember that gospel duties, including Christian education, can be built on nothing other than gospel foundation stones.

It is through the education of our children that our worldview is passed on to future generations and our civilization thereby preserved. Christians, therefore, have a very simple choice: either they educate their children in terms of godly learning and discipline and a Christian world-view, a covenantal, dominion-oriented worldview, and thereby help to build and preserve Christian civilization, or they hand over the education of their children to pagans who will educate them in terms of ungodly learning and discipline and a pagan worldview, and thereby help to build a pagan civilization which will enslave their children to the world they are called to rule over.[4]

As we undertake the education of our children, we are not on our own. We are accompanied by many great and precious promises.

29

A Pedagogic Creed

Foundations

I believe that people know themselves in knowing God, and that apart from confessing a true knowledge of God, they are in confusion and darkness. The God thus known must therefore be God as He reveals Himself in the created order, the holy Scriptures, and in our Lord Jesus Christ.

As Christian educators, we are to understand first who God is in His triune sovereignty, and secondly what He has done in the history of the created order—in the Creation, in the Incarnation, and in the final glory. In the light of who God is and what He has done, true education is possible. Outside that light, all attempts at education are fundamentally idolatrous and self-contradictory.

Love and Education

I believe that true education is a process of aiding baptized children to grow in their sanctification as they seek to love the Lord their God with all their heart, soul, mind, and strength, as God commands, and to love their neighbors as themselves.

Love is the greatest of all commands, not only in rank, but also in extent. No area of human existence can be found in which the command is not binding. Education is therefore the process of teaching little ones to love God in everything.

Covenant Kindness

I believe that the provision of a Christian education is one of the central covenant duties of Christian parents. These duties are not to be understood as works that men and women perform to earn anything in the sight of God, but rather as the natural response of faith in God's covenant promises. I further believe that God has promised His people that their children also belong to Him and that the fruition of this promise is appropriated by grace through faith. But as God's artwork, created in Christ Jesus to do good works that God prepared beforehand for us to do, we work out what He has worked into us. This outworking must include a faithful covenant education for our children.

PRETENDERS

I believe that the civil magistrate is established by God to be a ministry of justice and not a ministry of education. Therefore, as we seek to educate our children, the state has no part in this matter, whether direct or indirect. Consequently, I believe Christian educators should be wary of all civil promises, inducements, vouchers, incentives, or other entanglements. I further believe that a Christian child should never be abandoned to the government educators.

TEACHERS

I believe that teachers are all fallen in Adam and are sinners in need of redemption through the blood of Jesus Christ. Once they have been baptized, are walking with God as converted men and women, and have begun learning the lessons of Christ themselves, they may be trusted by godly parents *in loco parentis* to help provide a faithful covenant education to the children of the school.

And I believe that the chief qualification for such teachers is love—love for God, love for the parents who employ them, love for the students they teach, love for the subject matter they study and present, and love for the school.

STUDENTS

I believe that students are all fallen in Adam, and because they are sinners, they are in need of the salvation purchased by the Lord Jesus Christ. As baptized members of God's covenant people, they have a responsibility to learn the terms of the covenant—its history, its promises, its law, and its blessings and curses. As children under authority, they also have a responsibility to honor their parents and teachers who are faithfully discharging their covenant duties in teaching these things. And I believe that students must have this appropriate demeanor taught to them through word and example.

ANTITHESIS

I believe that because of the enmity God established between the seed of the woman and the seed of the serpent, all education has to emphasize the sharp divide between truth and error, goodness and sinfulness, loveliness and ugliness. Because the education we provide is being conducted in such a sinful world, one of the fundamental duties of all educators is to maintain a keen sense of the antithesis between right and wrong, good and evil. This task must be done at the broad cultural level as the teachers warn of the infidelity outside the faith. But it must also be done at the individual level as each teacher deals with the sinfulness of his or her own heart and the manifestations of sin among the students in the classroom.

A Christian school is not one in which sin has no access, but rather an educational setting where a group of Christians have resolved to understand sin biblically and deal with it accordingly.

TRIVIUM

I believe that God has created us in such a way that the children of our race, after they are born, grow naturally to maturity through three basic stages of learning. While in these stages, children display different strengths, which wise educators will utilize in their course of instruction. These strengths are, respectively, ability to memorize, argumentative acuity, and rhetorical sensitivity and presence.

I believe that the first stage (roughly ages five to twelve) corresponds to the grammar stage of the medieval Trivium. The second stage (roughly ages twelve to fourteen) corresponds to the dialectic stage of the Trivium. The third stage (roughly ages fourteen to eighteen) corresponds to the rhetoric stage of the Trivium.

Consequently, I believe that classes in the grammar stage should emphasize memorization, drill, chanting, and recitation. Classes in the dialectic stage should emphasize debate, explanation, analysis, and testing. Classes in the rhetoric stage should emphasize presentation and polish.

LIBERAL ARTS

I believe that training in the humanities is not, strictly speaking, a narrow vocational education at all, but rather training for life. As such, a foundational liberal education should be provided for every covenant child. Vocational training may begin at differing ages, according to the capacity of the child, but a basic liberal arts education should precede it. Every form of vocational training, to be genuinely Christian, should be built on the foundation of the Word.

A WESTERN CANON

I believe that every form of cultural egalitarianism is at the root a lie and is therefore mischievous in its effects on education. In the providence of God, the history of the kingdom of God and the history of Western civilization are intertwined. Born during the reign of Caesar Augustus, the Lord Jesus Christ sent out His apostles and emissaries to preach His Gospel to the uttermost parts of the earth. The first two thousand years of their obedience were spent largely to the north and west of Israel, and this has had cultural and historical consequences. This statement is not a cultural vaunt or boast, but is rather a recognition that the Gospel, and only the Gospel, displays such cultural power. I believe therefore that a truly Christian education will, with gratitude, emphasize the heritage of the West.

30

A CALL FOR TEACHERS

AS CHRISTIAN EDUCATORS, we are called to teach in difficult times. But our situation is greatly to be preferred to the dilemma of the unbelieving teacher, who is called to teach under impossible conditions. He is being called to make bricks without straw—*or* clay. Cornelius Van Til contrasts the position of the believing teacher with that of the unbeliever in a very powerful way:

> Authority is nothing but the placing of the absolute personality of God before the finite personality of man. It follows, then, that if nothing can be taught unless it is in relation to God, nothing can be taught unless it is taught with authority. It is this that makes the position of the teacher so infinitely difficult and at the same time so infinitely valuable. On the basis of our opponents the position of teacher is utterly hopeless. He knows that he knows nothing, and in spite of this he must teach. He knows that without authority he cannot teach and that there are no authorities to which he can appeal. He has to place the child before an infinite series of possibilities and pretend to be able to say something about the most advisable attitude to take with respect to those possibilities, and at the same time he has to admit that he knows nothing at all about those possibilities. And the result for the child is that he is not furnished with an atmosphere in which he can live and grow. In contrast with this, the Christian teacher knows himself, knows the subject, and knows the child. He has the full assurance of the absolute fruitfulness of his work. He labors in the dawn of everlasting results.[1]

Christian teachers labor in the dawn of everlasting results. They labor but with a good hope for the future. They hope for the future, but this hope is anchored with a realistic understanding of the work needed in the present. What better combination could there be in issuing a call for teachers? Paul tells us in two different places not to grow weary in doing that which is good (Gal. 6:9; 2 Thess. 3:13). He tells us this because we frequently do need the encouragement. Working as we are in these predawn hours, it is sometimes hard to see what we are doing. But look up—along the horizon is the radiant glow, what Van Til wonderfully called the dawn of everlasting results. How many children will stand up in that final day and bless your name as the instrumental cause of their presence there? To God be the glory, and amen, but every parent and every teacher should still hunger for the opportunity to say, as the Lord Jesus said, "Behold I and the children which God hath given me" (Heb. 2:13).

Unbelieving teachers may have new classrooms to teach in, under bright fluorescent lights. They are paid good salaries and are members of a powerful union. They have a retirement program. They have all the science equipment they want and brand-new textbooks all the time, filled with all the latest foolishness. And where is this well-funded education occurring? On the lip of an abyss, and much of the time is spent getting the kids to avoid looking in that direction.

We have to come to understand in our bones that in the long run moral rebellion and folly do not work. God's work done in God's way will always flourish under His blessing.

> It is only if we see that our ideal is the only rational ideal that we will be convinced that it will fully conquer in the end. It is that which gives us courage to labor on even though, as far as the immediate results are concerned, we seem to make little progress. . . . We need men and women on our teaching staffs that are intelligently unafraid. We need men and women on our teaching staffs who are confident of their own regeneration, who gladly work for the realization of an ideal that the world ridicules. We need men and women on our teaching staffs who understand the Christian philosophy of education, and also the anti-Christian philosophy of education that controls the pedagogy of our day. Such teachers will have the power of discrimination that is so all-important for their task. They will be able to take of the spoils of Egypt without afterwards yearning for the fleshpots of that false fatherland.[2]

Our task *is* difficult. We are trying to rebuild something that our fathers understood better than we do. I explained the dilemma in *Repairing the Ruins*: "The reason we need to rebuild is that we do not understand our heritage. We need to rebuild because of what we have lost; we do not know how to rebuild because we have lost it." We need to rebuild, but we have lost the blueprints.[3] We are trying to do all this with very little money and without fully understanding our task. We are trying to rebuild the ruins of Jerusalem with opponents taunting us about our (admitted!) inabilities in wall-building. They say that if a fox jumps on our wall, that wall will collapse; we wonder sometimes if it would take an animal that big.

But we are Christians nonetheless. "Christianity . . . offers no immediate panacea for the complex malady of the modern world. It has eternity before it, and it can afford to take its time."[4] In patience we are to possess our souls. One of the things I have said repeatedly at our education conferences, and which seems to resonate more than anything else, is that we want those laboring in the realm of Christian education reform to feel *simultaneously overwhelmed and encouraged*. This is only possible by the grace of God and will only come about if we seek to labor in the light of eternity.

We labor in this way, understanding that we are not the first to have done so. Moreover, we are not the first saints to be confronted with an educational mess. A case could actually be made that educational disorder is frequently the norm and that rebuilding the ruins is one of God's favorite assignments for His saints. The good news is that we are not educational inventors but rather educational historians.

> Outstanding teaching has existed in the world for millennia; we have no need to wait for the invention of anything new. The answers are in old and musty books, in the experiences of older teachers who have managed to ignore all the latest foolishness, and in a humble admission that while modernity does not know how to educate, our elders did. Modern education assumes the problem is in the student and spends a lot of time and money endlessly tinkering with him. Classical education assumes the problem is with our lust for innovation in teaching methods and strives to refine a tested adherence to the old.[5]

Our need for teachers is urgent, but the urgency should not make us lower our standards—the practice our generation has been following so disastrously. All this does is bring the profession under an even greater contempt and prevents good men and women from settling upon it as their calling under God. "We need the *best* men [and women] to teach our children. But the best are true Christians, who carry their religion into everything."[6] We need many more teachers than we currently have, and this is why we must expect far more from them. People have a way of living down to the standards set for them. But by the grace of God, in a time of reformation, they do the opposite.

We have a long way to go. The revelation of Scripture orients us and gives us our place in the world. The experience of our fathers in the past gives us a practical place to begin. With resources available, we ought to be doing far better than we are. At the same time, we must learn not to be discouraged, and we must learn to pray.

> *So teach us to number our days, that we may apply our hearts unto wisdom. Return, O LORD, how long? and let it repent thee concerning thy servants. O satisfy us early with thy mercy; that we may rejoice and be glad all our days. Make us glad according to the days wherein thou hast afflicted us, and the years wherein we have seen evil. Let thy work appear unto thy servants, and thy glory unto their children. And let the beauty of the LORD our God be upon us: and establish thou the work of our hands upon us; yea, the work of our hands establish thou it. (Ps. 90:12-17)*

Sheet-rocking classrooms, janitorial work, preparing lesson plans late at night, reading books way over our heads, driving ramshackle buses, coaching basketball teams, pulling teeth in the school office, starting schools when everyone said we were crazy, installing fire alarms—let the beauty of the Lord our God be upon us, and establish the work of our hands. Lord God, establish the work of our hands.

NOTES

CHAPTER ONE:
A MESS THAT JUST WON'T QUIT

1 Douglas Wilson, *The Paideia of God* (Moscow, Idaho: Canon Press, 1999), p. 115.

2 National School Safety Center: "School Safety Statistics," June 2001, p. 6 at nssc1.org

3 "How Dangerous Is Teaching in U.S. Schools?" on ABCNEWS.com

4 http://www.channel4000.com/news/stories/

5 *Insight, Washington Times* (October 1-8, 2001), p. 22.

6 Ibid.

7 *Washington Post*: "Back in Florida, Bush Pushes Education Plan" at http://www.washingtonpost.com

8 In the credit-where-credit's-due department, this is slightly better than it was in 1992. "The Nation's Report Card: Fourth Grade Reading 2000" (Executive Summary) found at http://nces.ed.gov/nationsreportcard/pubs/main2000/2001499.asp

9 ABCNEWS.com: "Faltering Middle Schools."

10 "Education at a Crossroads: What Works and What's Wasted in Education Today," report of the Subcommittee on Oversight and Investigations, Committee on Education and the Workforce, U.S. House of Representatives, 105th Cong., 2nd Sess., July 1998.

11 http://www.washingtonpost.com/ac2/wp-dyn/A99121-1998Feb25?language=printer

12 www.usatoday.com/usatonline/20020510/4101936s.htm

13 U.S. Department of Education, National Center for Education Statistics, at http://nces.ed.gov

14 National School Safety Center: "School Safety Statistics," June 2001, p. 3 at nssc1.org.

15 U.S. Department of Education, National Center for Education Statistics, *Digest of Education Statistics 2000*, Table 170.

16 Douglas Wilson, *Excused Absence* (Mission Viejo, Calif.: Crux Press, 2001), p. 81.

17 "NEA Goals, Spin and Concealment," *Phyllis Schlafly Report*, August 2001, p. 3 at http://www.eagleforum.org

18   Ibid., p. 4.

19   Ibid.

20   Ibid., p. 6.

21   R. L. Dabney, *On Secular Education* (Moscow, Idaho: Canon Press, 1989), p. 19.

22   Ibid., p. 24.

23   Robert Sweet, "Illiteracy: An Incurable Disease or Education Malpractice?" p. 3 at http://www.nrrf.org/essay_Illiteracy.html

24   Ibid., p. 7.

25   Ibid., p. 4.

26   U.S. Department of Education, National Center for Education Statistics, at http://nces.ed.gov

CHAPTER TWO:
THE RISE AND FALL OF SECULAR EDUCATION IN AMERICA

1   Douglas Wilson, *Repairing the Ruins* (Moscow, Idaho: Canon Press, 1996), p. 257.

2   Mortimer Adler, *Reforming Education: The Opening of the American Mind* (New York: Macmillan, Collier Books, 1977, 1988), p. 280.

3   Ibid., pp. 278-79.

4   Ibid., p. xxv.

5   Ibid., p. 249, emphasis mine.

6   Christopher Dawson, *The Crisis of Western Education* (Steubenville, Ohio: Franciscan University Press, 1989), p. 105.

7   Horace Mann, *Life and Works of Horace Mann, Vol. 3* (Boston: Lee and Shepard Publishers, 1891), p. 466.

8   Dawson, *The Crisis of Western Education*, p. 67.

9   R. L. Dabney, *On Secular Education* (Moscow, Idaho: Canon Press, 1989), pp. 26-27.

10   Ibid., p. 14.

11   Ibid., p. 15. Dabney is quoting John B. Minor.

12   Ibid., p. 25.

CHAPTER THREE:
HEALING THE WOUND LIGHTLY

1   Mortimer Adler, *Reforming Education: The Opening of the American Mind* (New York: Macmillan, Collier Books, 1977, 1988), p. 215.

2   Ibid., p. 44.

3   J. Gresham Machen, *Education, Christianity, and the State* (Jefferson, Md.: The Trinity Foundation, 1987), p. 50.

4   Douglas Wilson, *The Paideia of God* (Moscow, Idaho: Canon Press, 1999), p. 36.

5   http://heritage.org/library/backgrounder/bg1438es.html

6   Ibid.

7   *Citizen Magazine* Feature—"Charting the Way to School Reform," p. 2 found at http://www.family.org/cforum/citizenmag

8   Ibid., p. 8.

9   Wilson, *The Paideia of God*, p. 37.

10 Ibid., p. 34.

11 Ibid., p. 36.

12 Douglas Wilson, *Repairing the Ruins* (Moscow, Idaho: Canon Press, 1996), p. 231.

13 Ibid., p. 164.

CHAPTER FOUR:
THE NATURE OF MAN

1   David Stove, *Against the Idols of the Age* (London: Transaction Publishers, 1999), p. 139.

2   Horace Mann, *Life and Works of Horace Mann, Vol. 4* (Boston: Lee and Shepard Publishers, 1891), p. 140.

3   Mortimer J. Adler, *Reforming Education: The Opening of the American Mind* (New York: Macmillan, Collier Books, 1977, 1988), p. 13. It should be noted that Mortimer Adler embraced the Christian faith late in his life, but his work as a reformer in education was not informed by that later conversion.

4   Mann, *Life and Works, Vol. 2*, p. 50.

5   Adler, *Reforming Education*, p. 42.

6   Ibid., p. 15.

7   Douglas Jones, "Knowing Is Loving," in *Credenda/Agenda*, Vol. 14., No. 1.

8   Mann, *Life and Works, Vol. 2*, p. 81. Emphasis mine.

9   C. S. Lewis, *Poems* (New York: Harcourt Brace Jovanovich, 1964), p. 55.

10 Louis Berkhof and Cornelius Van Til, *Foundations of Christian Education: Addresses to Christian Teachers*, ed. Dennis E. Johnson (Phillipsburg, N.J.: Presbyterian and Reformed Publishing Co., 1990), p. 31.

11 Ibid., pp. 32-33.

12 Stephen C. Perks, *The Christian Philosophy of Education Explained* (Whitby, England: Avant Books, 1992), p. 89. Bob Dylan made this point during that brief time when he was making sense: "You gotta serve somebody."

13 Ibid., p. 47.

CHAPTER FIVE:
THE CASE AGAINST GOVERNMENT SCHOOLS

1   Cheri Fuller, in "Rebuilding Hope for Public Schools" at http://www.family.org/pplace/schoolkid/a0010291.cfm

2   Douglas Wilson, *Standing on the Promises* (Moscow, Idaho: Canon Press, 1997), p. 103.

3   Stephen C. Perks, *The Christian Philosophy of Education Explained* (Whitby, England: Avant Books, 1992), pp. 78-79.

4   Douglas Wilson, *Repairing the Ruins* (Moscow, Idaho: Canon Press, 1996), pp. 78-79.

5   Louis Berkhof and Cornelius Van Til, *Foundations of Christian Education: Addresses to Christian Teachers*, ed. Dennis E. Johnson (Phillipsburg, N.J.: Presbyterian and Reformed Publishing Co., 1990), p. 18.

6   Wilson, *Standing on the Promises*, p. 94.

7   Ibid., p. 94.

8   Perks, *Christian Philosophy of Education*, p. 116.

9   Douglas Wilson, *Excused Absence* (Mission Viejo, Calif.: Crux Press, 2001), p. 14.

10 Perks, *Christian Philosophy of Education*, p. 28.

11 Berkhof and Van Til, *Foundations of Christian Education*, p. 33.

12 Perks, *Christian Philosophy of Education*, pp. 115-16.

13 Berkhof and Van Til, *Foundations of Christian Education*, p. 77.

14 Lesslie Newbigin, *Foolishness to the Greeks* (Grand Rapids, Mich.: Eerdmans, 1986), p. 67.

CHAPTER SIX:
THE CENTRALITY OF WORSHIP

1   Jim Jordan, "The Case Against Western Civilization," found at http://www.biblicalhorizons.com. The article contains many thoughtful insights. The central criticism I would offer is that his insights appear to overlook the slow processes of cultural sanctification and show more than a little biblicist impatience. But yeast works through the loaf slowly.

2   Toby Sumpter, "Worship-Centered Education and the Role of the Church," unpublished paper.

CHAPTER SEVEN:
WHAT IS EDUCATION?

1   R. L. Dabney, *On Secular Education* (Moscow, Idaho: Canon Press, 1989), p. 13.

2   Louis Berkhof and Cornelius Van Til, *Foundations of Christian Education: Addresses to Christian Teachers*, ed. Dennis E. Johnson (Phillipsburg, N.J.: Presbyterian and Reformed Publishing Co., 1990), p. 44.

3   Stephen C. Perks, *The Christian Philosophy of Education Explained* (Whitby, England: Avant Books, 1992), p. 63.

4   Berkhof and Van Til, *Foundations of Christian Education*, p. 18.

5   Ibid., p. 4.

6   Mortimer Adler, *Reforming Education: The Opening of the American Mind* (New York: Macmillan, Collier Books, 1977, 1988), p. 328.

7   Ibid., p. 110.

8   C. S. Lewis, *The Great Divorce* (New York: Macmillan, 1957), p. 37.

9   Berkhof and Van Til, *Foundations of Christian Education*, p. 116.

10 Ibid., p. 81.

11 Foreword by R. V. Young, in Christopher Dawson, *The Crisis of Western Education* (Steubenville, Ohio: Franciscan University Press, 1989), p. xxii.

12 Berkhof and Van Til, *Foundations of Christian Education*, p. 81.

CHAPTER EIGHT:
DEMOCRACY AND EGALITARIANISM

1   Douglas Jones and Douglas Wilson, *Angels in the Architecture* (Moscow, Idaho: Canon Press, 1998), p. 166.

2   C. S. Lewis, *The Screwtape Letters* (New York: Macmillan, 1962), p. 169.

3   Horace Mann, *Life and Works of Horace Mann, Vol. 4* (Boston: Lee and Shepard Publishers, 1891), p. 133.

4   Ibid., *Vol. 3*, pp. 417-18. Capitalization and emphasis are the author's.

5   Ibid., *Vol. 4*, p. 220.

6   Ibid., *Vol. 2*, p. 83.

7   Ibid., *Vol. 4*, p. 116.

8   Mortimer Adler, *Reforming Education: The Opening of the American Mind* (New York: Macmillan, Collier Books, 1977, 1988), p. 107.

9   Ibid., p. 111.

CHAPTER NINE:
WHAT IS CLASSICAL EDUCATION?

1   Gene Edward Veith, Jr., and Andrew Kern, *Classical Education: The Movement Sweeping America* (Washington D.C.: Capital Research Center, 2001), p. 26.

2   "Thomas Jefferson School Curriculum Guide." The school is located at 4100 South Lindbergh Boulevard, St. Louis, MO 63127.

3   Veith and Kern, *Classical Education*, p. 33-34.

4   Ibid., p. 36.

5   Ibid., p. 40.

CHAPTER TEN:
LOGOS SCHOOL, ACCS, AND NEW ST. ANDREWS

1   More information can be obtained by writing to ACCS, P.O. Box 9741, Moscow, ID 83843.

2   Phone: 1-208-883-3199. Their website is at logosschool.com.

3   Their website is canonpress.org, and a catalog can be requested by calling 1-800-488-2034.

4   Veritas can be called at 1-800-922-5082 or e-mailed at Veritasprs@aol.com.

5   Douglas Wilson, *The Paideia of God* (Moscow, Idaho: Canon Press, 1999), pp. 113ff.

CHAPTER ELEVEN:
THE CHRISTIAN HEART AND MIND

1   Douglas Wilson, *The Paideia of God* (Moscow, Idaho: Canon Press, 1999), p. 131.

2   Douglas Wilson, *Repairing the Ruins* (Moscow, Idaho: Canon Press, 1996), p. 170.

3   R. L. Dabney, *On Secular Education* (Moscow, Idaho: Canon Press, 1989), p. 22.

4   Mortimer Adler, *Reforming Education: The Opening of the American Mind* (New York: Macmillan, Collier Books, 1977, 1988), p. 179, emphasis mine.

5   Dabney, *On Secular Education*, p. 17.

CHAPTER TWELVE:
THE PEERS PROBLEM

1   A Nehemiah Publication, "The PEERS Test: Biblical Worldview Testing and Training," Nehemiah Institute, Lexington, Ky., 1994, pamphlet.

2   Ibid.

3   Ibid., p. 3.

4   A Nehemiah Publication, "PEERS Trend Chart," Nehemiah Institute, Lexington, Ky., 2000.

5   Dan Smithwick, "One School Generation to Go, and Then the End," Nehemiah Institute, Lexington, Ky., 2001, paper.

6   Dan Smithwick, *A "World" of Difference in Public and Christian Schools* (Lexington, Ky.: The Nehemiah Institute, 1999), p. 17.

7   A Nehemiah Publication, "Baptist Church Schools: Special Study of 60 Schools," Nehemiah Institute, Lexington, Ky., 2000, chart.

CHAPTER THIRTEEN:
THE *PAIDEIA* OF GOD

1   Douglas Wilson, *The Paideia of God* (Moscow, Idaho: Canon Press, 1999), p. 11.

2   Werner Jaeger, *Paideia: The Ideals of Greek Culture, Vol. 3* (Oxford: Oxford University Press, 1944), p. 314.

3   Christopher Dawson, *The Crisis of Western Education* (Steubenville, Ohio: Franciscan University Press, 1989), p. 8.

4   Ibid., p. 9.

5   Ibid., p. 8.

6   Werner Jaeger, *Early Christianity and Greek Paideia* (Cambridge: Belknap Press, Harvard University, 1961), pp. 117-18.

7   Dawson, *The Crisis of Western Education*, p. 135.

CHAPTER FOURTEEN:
THE SEVEN LIBERAL ARTS

1   John Henry Cardinal Newman, *The Idea of a University* (Garden City, N.Y.: Image Books, 1959), p. 253.

2   Christopher Dawson, *The Making of Europe* (New York: Meridian Books, 1956), p. 59.

3   S. E. Frost, Jr., *Historical and Philosophical Foundations of Western Education* (Columbus, Ohio: Charles Merrill Books, 1966), p. 36.

4   Frank Graves, *A History of Education Before the Middle Ages* (New York: Macmillan, 1931), p. 125.

5   Frost, *Historical and Philosophical Foundations*, p. 37.

6   Graves, *A History of Education Before the Middle Ages*, p. 124.

7   Ibid., p. 125.

8   Frost, *Historical and Philosophical Foundations*, p. 40.

9   Graves, *A History of Education Before the Middle Ages*, p. 126.

10   Ibid., p. 127.

11   Ibid., p. 130.

12   Frost, *Historical and Philosophical Foundations*, p. 102.

13   Edward Power, *A Legacy of Learning* (Albany, N.Y.: SUNY Press, 1991), p. 114.

14   William Boyd, *The History of Western Education* (London: Adam and Charles Black, 1921), pp. 102-03.

15   Frank Graves, *A History of Education During the Middle Ages and the Transition to Modern Times* (New York: Macmillan, 1910), p. 27.

16   A. T. Drane, *Christian Schools and Scholars* (New York: G. E. Stechert & Co., 1910), pp. 31-32.

17   Henri de Lubac, *Medieval Exegesis* (Grand Rapids: Eerdmans, 1998), p. 216.

18   Power, *A Legacy of Learning*, p. 113.

19   Lubac, *Medieval Exegesis*, p. 215.

20   Ibid., p. 44.

21   Ibid.

22   Graves, *A History of Education During the Middle Ages*, p. 15, 17.

23   Ibid., p. 27.

24   Ibid., p. 115.

25   Frost, *Historical and Philosophical Foundations*, p. 175.

26   Graves, *A History of Education During the Middle Ages*, p. 146.

27   Boyd, *History of Western Education*, p. 171 .

28   Ibid., p. 184.

29   Frost, *Historical and Philosophical Foundations*, p. 177.

30   Graves, *A History of Education During the Middle Ages*, p. 51.

31   John Comenius, *John Amos Comenius* (Switzerland: UNESCO, 1957), p. 100.

32   Ibid., p. 78.

33   Ibid., p. 13.

34   M. W. Keatinge, *The Great Didactic of John Amos Comenius* (London: Adam and Charles Black, 1896), p. 148.

35   Ibid., pp. 125-26.

36   Ibid., p. 125.

37   Graves, *A History of Education During the Middle Ages*, p. 186.

38   Keatinge, *The Great Didactic*, p. 108.

39   Boyd, *History of Western Education*, p. 198.

40   Graves, *A History of Education During the Middle Ages*, p. 193.

41   Keatinge, *The Great Didactic*, pp. 133-34. Also see Graves, *A History of Education During the Middle Ages*, p. 194.

42   Boyd, *History of Western Education*, p. 201.

43   Ibid., pp. 272-73.

44   Christopher Dawson, *The Crisis of Western Education* (Steubenville, Ohio: Franciscan University Press, 1989), p. 37.

45   Samuel Eliot Morison, *The Intellectual Life of Colonial New England* (Ithaca, N.Y.: Great Seal Books, 1956), p. 17.

46   Dawson, *The Crisis of Western Education*, p. 135.

47   Ibid., p. 156.

48   Ibid., p. 136.

49   Ibid., p. 188.

50 Ibid., p. 152.

51 Ibid., p. 204.

CHAPTER FIFTEEN:
THE TRIVIUM

1 In this section, I am greatly indebted to Randy Booth's essay "The Trivium in Biblical Perspective," *The Classis*, Vol. 4, No. 1, January 1997.

CHAPTER SIXTEEN:
A CASE FOR LATIN

1 Colin Gunton, *The One, The Three and the Many* (Cambridge: Cambridge University Press, 1993), p. 171.

2 *Latin and Greek in American Education: With Symposia on the Value of Humanistic Studies*, ed. Francis W. Kelsey (New York: Macmillan, 1911), p. 21.

3 Ibid., p. 327.

4 Ibid., p. 167.

5 Ibid., p. 162.

6 Ibid., p. 32l.

7 Ibid., p. 25.

8 Ibid., p. 237.

9 Christopher Dawson, *The Crisis of Western Education* (Steubenville, Ohio: Franciscan University Press, 1989), p. 11.

10 *Latin and Greek in American Education*, p. 157.

CHAPTER SEVENTEEN:
WHAT CLASSICAL IS NOT

1 Charles Spurgeon, *Teaching Children* (Pasadena, Texas: Pilgrim Publications, n.d.), p. 10.

2 St. Augustine, *On Christian Teaching* (Oxford: Oxford University Press, 1997), p. 105.

3 Ibid., p. 102.

4 Jeremy Wilkins, "What's in a Grade?" *Ennui*, Fall 2001.

5 Augustine, *On Christian Teaching*, p. 117.

CHAPTER EIGHTEEN:
EDUCATING THE IMAGINATION

1 C. S. Lewis, *Christian Reflections* (Grand Rapids: Eerdmans, 1967), p. 93.

2   Douglas Wilson, Wes Callihan, and Douglas Jones, *Classical Education and the Homeschool* (Moscow, Idaho: Canon Press, 2001), p. 22.

3   Douglas Wilson, *The Paideia of God* (Moscow, Idaho: Canon Press, 1999), p. 23.

4   Thomas Peters, *The Christian Imagination* (San Francisco: Ignatius Press, 2000), p. 10.

5   Douglas Wilson, *Repairing the Ruins* (Moscow, Idaho: Canon Press, 1996), pp. 168-69.

6   Ibid., p. 168.

7   Ibid., p. 165.

8   Wilson, Callihan, and Jones, *Classical Education and the Homeschool*, pp. 19-20.

9   Ibid., p. 20.

10 Wilson, *The Paideia of God*, p. 78.

CHAPTER NINETEEN:
CLASSICAL ATHLETICS

1   Frank Graves, *A History of Education During the Middle Ages and the Transition to Modern Times* (New York: Macmillan, 1910), p. 186. In submission to Scripture, gymnastics certainly benefit both body and soul.

CHAPTER TWENTY-ONE:
BOARDSMANSHIP

1   C. S. Lewis, *Prince Caspian* (New York: Macmillan, 1951), p. 92.

2   Douglas Wilson, *Repairing the Ruins* (Moscow, Idaho: Canon Press, 1996), p. 201.

3   Bobb Biehl and Ted Ingstrom, *Increasing Your Boardroom Confidence* (Phoenix: Questar Publishers, 1988). I am indebted to Biehl and Ingstrom for this helpful distillation of a board's duties.

CHAPTER TWENTY-TWO:
SCHOOL CLOTHES

1   Douglas Wilson, *The Paideia of God* (Moscow, Idaho: Canon Press, 1999), p. 39.

2   Ibid., pp. 48-49.

3   St. Augustine, *On Christian Teaching* (Oxford: Oxford University Press, 1997), p. 136.

CHAPTER TWENTY-THREE:
THE SEVEN LAWS OF TEACHING

1   John Milton Gregory, *The Seven Laws of Teaching* (Grand Rapids, Mich.: Baker Book House, 1979).

2   Ibid., p. 30.

3   Ibid., p. 33.

4   Ibid., p. 44.

5   Ibid., p. 54.

6   Ibid., p. 67.

7   Ibid., p. 84.

8   Ibid., p. 87.

9   Ibid., p. 101.

10   Ibid., p. 107.

11   Ibid., p. 113.

CHAPTER TWENTY-FOUR:
ALTERNATIVES TO SCHOOL

1   *Time* magazine, August 27, 2001.

2   Douglas Wilson, Wes Callihan, Douglas Jones, *Classical Education and the Homeschool* (Moscow, Idaho: Canon Press, 2001).

3   Douglas Wilson, *Future Men* (Moscow, Idaho: Canon Press, 2001), pp. 113-15.

CHAPTER TWENTY-FIVE:
THE THREAT OF STATE ENTANGLEMENT

1   See "Unstoppable Choice?" *World* magazine, September 8, 2001, p. 22.

2   Nathan Wilson, "Voucher Envy," *Credenda/Agenda*, vol. 10, no. 3.

CHAPTER TWENTY-SEVEN:
CANONICAL BOOKS

1   For a good Christian introduction to many of these books and others besides, see Louise Cowan and Os Guinness, *Invitation to the Classics* (Grand Rapids, Mich.: Baker, 1998).

2   Douglas Wilson, *Mother Kirk* (Moscow, Idaho: Canon Press, 2001), pp. 51-60.

3   C. S. Lewis, *God in the Dock* (Grand Rapids, Mich.: Eerdmans, 1970), p. 206. That test was the fact that Athanasius was able to write on such a deep subject with classical simplicity.

4   Joseph Sobran, *Alias Shakespeare* (New York: Free Press, 1997).

5   C. S. Lewis, *A Preface to Paradise Lost* (London: Oxford University, 1970).

6   C. S. Lewis, *The Quotable Lewis* (Wheaton, Ill.: Tyndale, 1989), p. 81.

7   Cowan and Guinness, *Invitation to the Classics*, p. 283.

CHAPTER TWENTY-EIGHT:
AND UNTO CHILDREN'S CHILDREN

1   Douglas Wilson, *Standing on the Promises* (Moscow, Idaho: Canon Press, 1997), p. 24.

2   Ibid., p. 23.

3   Louis Berkhof and Cornelius Van Til, *Foundations of Christian Education: Addresses to Christian Teachers*, ed. Dennis E. Johnson (Phillipsburg, N.J.: Presbyterian and Reformed Publishing Co., 1990), p. 29.

4   Stephen C. Perks, *The Christian Philosophy of Education Explained* (Whitby, England: Avant Books, 1992), pp. 115-16.

CHAPTER THIRTY:
A CALL FOR TEACHERS

1   Louis Berkhof and Cornelius Van Til, *Foundations of Christian Education: Addresses to Christian Teachers*, ed. Dennis E. Johnson (Phillipsburg, N.J.: Presbyterian and Reformed Publishing Co., 1990), p. 24.

2   Ibid., pp. 99-100.

3   Douglas Wilson, *Repairing the Ruins* (Moscow, Idaho: Canon Press, 1996), p. 260.

4   Christopher Dawson, *The Crisis of Western Education* (Steubenville, Ohio: Franciscan University Press, 1989), p. 144.

5   Douglas Wilson, *The Paideia of God* (Moscow, Idaho: Canon Press, 1999), pp. 28-29.

6   R. L. Dabney, *On Secular Education* (Moscow, Idaho: Canon Press, 1989), p. 21, emphasis mine.

INDEX

Scripture Index